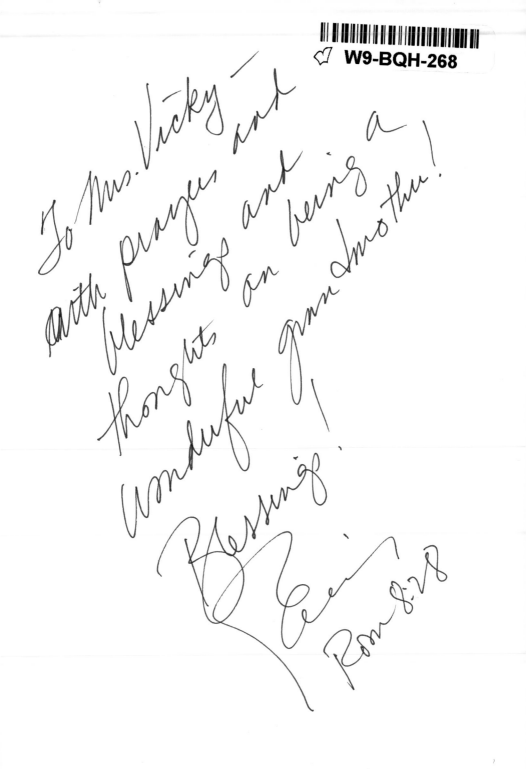

To Mrs. Vicky —
with prayers and
blessings and being a
thoughts on being a
wonderful grandmother!

Blessings,
[signature]
Rom 8:28

The Grandparent Factor

The Grandparent Factor

Five Principles to Help You Make a Difference
In the Life of Your Grandchild

PHIL WALDREP WITH **PAT SPRINGLE**

FOREWORD BY ART LINKLETTER

Published in the United States by Baxter Press, Friendswood, Texas.
Cover design by Ruth Bochte, Phil Waldrep Ministries, Trinity, Alabama.
Formatted by Anne McLaughlin, Blue Lake Design, Dickinson, Texas.
Edited by Stan Campbell, Hendersonville, Tennessee.

ISBN: 1-888237-44-9

The version of the Bible used in this book is the *New King James Version*.

A grandmother is a lady who has no children of her own, so she likes other people's little girls. A grandfather is a man grandmother. He goes for walks with the boys and they talk about fishing and tractors and like that. Grandmas don't have to do anything except be there. They're old, so they shouldn't play hard or run. It is enough if they drive us to the market where the pretend horse is and have lots of dimes ready. Or if they take us for walks, they should slow down past things like pretty leaves or caterpillars. They should never ever say "hurry up." Usually they are fat, but not too fat to tie kids' shoes. They wear glasses and funny underwear. They can take their teeth out and gums off.

It is better if they don't typewrite or play cards except with us. They don't have to be smart, only answer questions like why dogs hate cats and how come God isn't married. They don't talk baby talk like visitors do, because it is hard to understand. When they read to us they don't skip, or mind if it is the same old story again.

Everybody should try to have one, especially if you don't have television, because grandmas are the only grown-ups who have got time.

—A nine-year-old girl's description of her grandparents

Table of Contents

❧

Acknowledgments

A few years ago I made an amazing discovery as I sat on the platform for one of our senior adult celebrations. Earlier that day I had a discussion with a group of people about the problems their community was having with teenagers. Many of the group surmised that the parents of these adolescents simply did not care. They also believed their churches were indifferent and their schools were powerless to make a change in the lives of young people.

My mind wandered during the program that evening as I contemplated their remarks. Then it suddenly occurred to me: These retired adults were the answer! They had the time and the energy to make a difference! But apparently, the thought never crossed their minds to become an agent of change. If I had suggested they become the solution to the problem they were raising, they probably would have found plenty of reasons to reject my assertion. So, I returned home to test my theory and prove my point before making any recommendations.

I first talked with a police officer that works with juvenile delinquents. I asked him if these teens ever mentioned an adult who they trusted and who influenced them for good. Without hesitation, he told me that nearly every juvenile delinquent – he could think of no exceptions – admired and respected at least one grandparent. A guidance counselor at a local school confirmed the comments of the law enforcement officer. In fact, the counselor said she often tried to involve a grandparent when a student needed an adult accountability partner. Finally, a friend who works in a community program that provides recreational opportunities to local kids agreed. He said he had great hope for any boy or girl from a troubled home who had at least one grandparent who cared enough to be involved.

My guess was right. The secret weapon for changing the outlook and future of today's children is a grandparent who sees himself or herself as an influential force in the life of that grandchild. This book seeks to help grandparents know what their grandchildren desperately need.

What is your grandchild looking for? What is his or her basic need? How can you, as a grandparent, effectively meet that child's changing emotional needs?

Grandparents cannot completely replace a godly father or mother, but they can fill a void caused by the emotional neglect or absence of a parent. That's the message of this book.

No book is the sole work of one author. Through the experiences of life and interaction with others, many people make valuable contributions to a person's life, and then, to any written work. Such is the case with this book. I want to thank these people for shaping my life and this message:

First, to my parents, Linnes and Burnell Waldrep, and to my mother-in-law, Jane Gray, who are the best grandparents my kids could have. And to my father-in-law, Richard Gray, who went to be with the Lord several years ago but who contributed so much to all of our lives. How proud he would be of all his grandchildren if he could be with them now!

To my only living grandparent, Linnie Cross, who, at 92 years of age, continues to be a positive factor in my life.

To my extended family who encourage and pray for our ministry and me.

To the Board of Directors of the Phil Waldrep Evangelistic Association who give valuable insight and guidance to our work.

To Barry, Tina, Susan, Marla, Ruth and Duck – the best staff in the world – who are hard workers and among my best friends.

To our graphic artist, Ruth Bochte, who designed the cover and selected the photographs for the book, and to Charlie Seifried of Charlie Seifried Photography for the use of his photographs. You both never cease to amaze me with your talents and your ability to raise creativity to a new level.

To Mike Anderson, the staff and the boys and girls of the North Alabama Boys and Clubs who offered their time and insight that confirmed or challenged many of the concepts of this book.

To my pastor, Dr. Mark Tolbert, and the staff and members of Central Baptist Church in Decatur, Alabama, for their continued love, encouragement and support.

To the pastors, churches and ministries who partner with us to make a difference in the lives of people.

To my friend, Pat Springle, who uses his gifts and skills to help me clearly express my thoughts and ideas.

And, most importantly, to my wife, Debbie, and our two daughters, Maegan and Melodi, who make my life as a husband and dad a joy.

Finally, to every grandparent who reads this book, I offer a sincere prayer that these words will help you make a real difference in the lives of your grandchildren, one that will make you a positive factor in their lives.

Phil Waldrep
January 7, 2003
Trinity, Alabama

Foreword

It is my pleasure to recommend Phil's book to you. I have known Phil for several years, and I trust his godly insights about how we grandparents can have a wonderful influence on our grandkids. This book is full of principles to guide our actions, and it is filled with hope to encourage our hearts.

I've interviewed thousands of people in my lifetime, and I've realized that the two most interesting groups of people are kids 4 to 10 and adults over 65. They both say some outrageous things. The youngsters often don't know what they're saying, and the older ones don't care.

Years ago on my show, "House Party," I asked a little boy what he would like to take with him if he went to heaven in the next few weeks. He said, "I'd like to take my Mother and Dad." I asked him, "Why would you want to take them?" He replied with a straight face, "I think up there they'd have more time for me."

The American family is in turmoil. Divorce, mobility, stress, and the frantic pace of life have ripped the fabric of relationships for many adults and children. Grandparents could step into this void, but many grandparents today spend very little time with their grandkids. Sometimes they live far away from each other; sometimes the parents are too busy to make time for this crucial relationship between grandparents and grandchildren; and sometimes either the grandparents or the kids are preoccupied with their own lives and don't value each other as much as they might.

We have all kinds of modern communication technologies, including cell phones, email, instant messaging, and digital cameras, and we hope those things will fill the void in young people's hearts. But technology can't replace hugs, words of kindness, and time spent with a loving grandparent. Ironically, as the average life span increases and grandparents live longer, healthier lives, they have an even greater opportunity to have a powerfully positive impact on their grandchildren—and their great-grandchildren. But the fracturing of the family means grandparents will need to make a more concerted effort to have such an influence.

When I was a child, my parents abandoned me. In fact, I never have known who they were. The newspapers in that little town, Moosejaw, Saskatchewan, printed an article about a baby boy who had been abandoned by his parents. An old Baptist preacher, Fulton John Linkletter, and his wife were in the town on an evangelistic tour. They read the article about the baby who had been left behind, and they adopted me. Instantly, I became a preacher's kid. There are certainly some benefits of being the child of a preacher, but there are liabilities, too. At meals, my father prayed, and I mean, he prayed for every missionary in every corner of the globe. He prayed so long that I was 14 before a bite of hot food passed my lips!

My Dad was old and crippled, so he wasn't able to take me camping, swimming, and hiking, but he took me to the YMCA near our home in San Diego where I could be actively involved with wonderful young Christians. Some of the people who had the most significant influence in my life were the YMCA directors. My creativity wasn't a threat to them. Instead, they encouraged me to try all kinds of things, and their encouragement brought out talents I didn't even know I had.

For instance, the directors asked me to be a YMCA camp leader in the backcountry near San Diego, and they asked me to be in charge of entertainment. I learned to organize kids' campfire programs, and I became a program director and an emcee. In addition, my involvement with those leaders in the YMCA gave me a deep appreciation for sportsmanship, honesty, and integrity. Their optimism and sense of honor was a tremendous example for me, and their encouragement proved to be instrumental in shaping my character and my career. With the confidence I received from these experiences, I took the next step in college and wrote plays and musical comedies, which ultimately led me into a career in broadcasting.

Every child needs an older adult as a source of encouragement and a powerful example of hope and optimism. My parents and those YMCA directors did that for me. Grandparents are in a position to play such a vital role in the lives of their grandchildren.

Some of us grandparents have experienced tremendous hurts that can change our lives—for good or ill. If we fail to turn to God and open our hearts to His goodness and insights, our painful experiences can cause us to become bitter, sour, and demanding. But if, in the most painful times of our lives, we experience God's goodness and grace, we develop wisdom and compassion, and we become wonderfully approachable people.

Several years ago, my youngest daughter, Diane, jumped to her death when someone gave her the hallucinogenic drug, LSD. She was not a bad girl, just an adventurous one. I was in Colorado Springs preparing to give the commencement address at the Air Force Academy when I got the news that devastated our family. That event, I was certain, was going to change my life, but I was determined that it would change me for the better.

After my initial anger, dismay, and guilt—which are normal in any death of a loved one, especially a suicide—I had a choice. I could choose to be *diminished* by blaming myself or God and becoming suspicious and bitter, or I could choose to be *enhanced* by trusting that God's plan is far above anything we can possibly imagine and that He would ultimately use the painful event for good. Instead of remaining self-absorbed in my grief and guilt, I chose to become active in national and international drug abuse prevention. I was on the President's Council on Drug Policy, and I spoke to the United Nations to encourage them to make a difference in the lives of men and women, young and old, throughout the world. Did my grief go away? No, not for a long, long time, but God enabled me to use the pain as a fuel to do something positive in the lives of others.

If you have lived long enough to be a grandparent, you have experienced loving relationships and fantastic events. You have many fond memories. But you have also experienced some traumatic and painful events. Don't let those hurts keep you self-absorbed. Trust God to use them to strengthen you and make you even more useful, a source of strength and hope in the lives of those who look up to you. We may not be able to stop hardening of the arteries, but we can stop hardening of the attitudes. Be a deep well of hope for your grandchildren.

My wife and I had five children, seven grandchildren, and 14 great-grandchildren. Our clan is spread throughout the country and the world, including San Diego, Seattle, New York, Indonesia, and other places. All of us are busy and are sinking our roots deep into the communities where we live, but we also believe it is vitally important that we stay connected as a family. Keeping our family strong is so important that I bring them all together once a year for a week when we can laugh, talk, cry, and remain an irreplaceable part of each other's lives. Fitting this week into our busy schedules is difficult for some of us, but all of us realize that we desperately need this time together. It is in those days, those hours, and those precious moments that we can look into each other's eyes and touch each other's hearts. Those moments are well worth all the time, expense, and effort.

If you are a grandparent, you have the incredible privilege of touching the lives of your grandkids. The fracturing of the family may make relating to them more difficult, but it is more necessary today than ever before. Whatever your resources of time, money, and energy may be, use them to connect in meaningful ways with your grandchildren. Their lives will be richer because you do. And yours will, too.

Art Linkletter
Host of *House Party* for 26 years, on which he interviewed over 27,000 children from ages 4 to 10; producer of *Kids Say the Darndest Things* with host Bill Cosby; president of the Center on Aging at the UCLA Medical School

You Can Make a Difference!

*"Woe to him who is alone when he falls,
for he has no one to help him up" (Ecclesiastes 4:10).*

A few years ago, my friend Brad Jones and I were in Montana to speak at a church each night for a week. On Tuesday night, the church had planned a pizza party for the young people and their friends. Before we left the hotel to go to the church that evening, I was watching the news. The reporter led with a story about a shooting in a high school, following it with details about the recent rash of violence in high schools around the nation: Columbine, Kentucky, Georgia, California, and on and on.

As I watched, I was gripped with horror. More than ever, I was determined to find a solution for this recurring problem. As the reporter continued, my mind raced through ideas about helping parents be better role models, training teachers to identify problem kids, providing schools with metal detectors, sponsoring assemblies and conflict resolution seminars, reinstituting corporal punishment, putting permissive parents in jail, and all kinds of other things—most of which had already been implemented and seemed to be relatively ineffective in quelling the violence. "How in the world," I wondered, "are we going to solve this problem of violence in the schools?" The more I thought about it, the more hopeless I felt. If this trend continues, I concluded, every child will need a bodyguard to go to school. That's ridiculous, but it's becoming a reality.

A few minutes later, Brad and I got in the car to drive to the church. I began pouring out my frustrations and feelings of hopelessness about the problem of violence in the schools. I told him about all the ideas I had, but admitted that none of them offered much promise. Brad listened patiently (probably because I didn't give him much of a chance to say anything) until my verbal tank finally ran dry. Then he smiled and said, "I think I've got the answer."

"I think I've got the answer."

"You do? What is it?"

He smiled again and said, "I'll show you tonight."

About that time, we pulled into the church parking lot and got out of the car. A girl who was about 12 years old spotted us, ran over, and gave Brad a huge hug.

Brad smiled and said, "Hey, Suzanne!"

"Come with me," she grinned. "I want you to meet my grandmother."

Suzanne took Brad by the hand and led him into the church. He nodded for me to follow them. The young girl excitedly introduced Brad to her grandmother, Rachel, and then Brad introduced me. As we exchanged a few pleasant remarks, scores of young people—very hungry young people—began arriving. A few minutes later, the delivery boys walked in with stacks of pizza boxes, and the feeding frenzy was on! Rachel and I found seats next to each other away from the noise of the young people all talking and chewing at the same time.

I started our conversation by asking, "Rachel, tell me about your granddaughter."

Rachel winced a bit as she began. "She's had a hard life. Her dad left Ruth, my daughter, but Ruth is trying her very best to make a good life for Suzanne. Ruth has a job and she works hard, but other kids sometimes make Suzanne feel bad because she doesn't have a dad at home." Rachel paused a moment and continued, "She's had some struggles in school. Her grades haven't been too good. In addition, she doesn't feel that she's as pretty as some of her friends, and at her age, that's a major concern."

As Rachel talked, I realized that Suzanne had all the potential in the world to feel like a loser: no dad, busy mom, poor student, not attractive, and a victim of cruel kids' taunts. Most people in her position don't get a gun and go to school to kill those who taunt her, but many others do become social misfits for the rest of their lives. Yet Suzanne's young, eager face didn't reflect any such possibilities. No, she was a happy person—thrilled, actually—enjoying her friends, talking and laughing, and as secure as any junior high student I've ever seen. What was the difference, I wondered, between Suzanne and countless other young people who become violent or depressed?

I asked Rachel, "I noticed that Suzanne certainly has a genuine smile. How do you explain her happiness?"

Rachel laughed softly, "Well, I'm not sure I have the answer to that question, but I'll tell you this: As her grandmother, I've made it my goal to make a difference in her life. I spend as much time as possible with her every day. I tell her how proud I am of her and how pretty she is. And we hug a lot." She thought for a moment. "I'm not trying to be her surrogate father, but I want to be the best grandmother I can be for that precious little girl. I want to be a positive factor in her life."

> *"I want to be the best grandmother I can be for that precious little girl. I want to be a positive factor in her life."*

Brad was right. He had shown me an answer. One of the solutions to the problems facing young people is the loving involvement of their grandparents. Attentive grandparents can be, as Rachel said, "a factor" that shapes youngsters powerfully and positively for the rest of their lives. I've talked to hundreds of grandparents across the country since then, and I'm convinced that many of them want to answer that high calling with firm commitment, clear understanding, time, sacrifice, and courage.

NEEDS, SEEN AND UNSEEN

Some of the distresses in the lives of young people are evident because we see them each day on the evening news and the morning papers: school violence, drug addiction, unwanted pregnancies, gangs, murder, runaways, driving under the influence, and a host of other calamities. Some people have grandchildren who make these headlines, but most don't. Yet their own grandchildren may be among those in whom rage and depression simmer under the surface and only occasionally explode or implode.

Developmental psychologists tell us that adolescents are defining and establishing their identity. They are trying to answer crucial questions: *Who am I? Where do I belong? What can I contribute?*

The influence of parents often contradicts the influence of peers as young people struggle through the process of becoming individuals—adults instead of children. That process is exciting, but it leaves them vulnerable, easily hurt, and impulsive, which may lead to unwise decisions. In the fishbowl of adolescent relationships, every action and every word is scrutinized by others, and harshly condemned if someone doesn't measure up as sharp or cool.

A massive infusion of hormones can also cloud thinking during this personal quest for self-identity. Developing bodies add to the explosive equation of excitement and instability. Those who are beautiful or handsome are praised; those who lack such qualities are often viciously ridiculed and rejected.

Family problems often add to the pressures. As young people reach adolescence, their parents may be in a stage of reevaluating their own lives. The excitement and stability of earlier years of marriage may have deteriorated into bland sameness and boredom, or perhaps even attempts to find excitement in other arms or new pursuits. Financial burdens of raising teenagers can contribute to the level of stress in the family and make parents less patient during a time when more patience is needed.

Many young people live with a constant, nagging fear that they simply don't fit in at school or at home. They may smile, laugh, and be involved in all kinds of activities, yet they remain terribly insecure underneath their masks. Sooner or later, most young people mature and develop a strong sense of identity as young adults. Too many, however, feel the crushing weight of expectations from the opposite sex, from their friends, from parents, from teachers, and from an even stricter critic: themselves. They react in anger, withdraw in hopelessness, or cycle between these two extremes. They don't feel accepted, so they reject those who are rejecting them.

> *Many young people live with a constant, nagging fear that they simply don't fit in at school or at home.*

Younger children are developing, too, but in different ways. They don't yet feel the powerful surge of hormones, the need to answer life's biggest questions, and the quest for individuality. They aren't old enough to drive, so they require more parental involvement. They need time and attention to help them in school and with their friends, and they also need to be taken to games, practice, plays, school, and all the other activities that have become a part of modern life. If they don't get the attention they need, they can become just as angry or depressed as adolescents, yet the expression of their powerful emotions may not be as volatile.

Parents are often preoccupied with their own struggles during these crucial years, and instead of offering understanding and guidance, they add to the demands and the sense of isolation in their kids. Parents come home tired after a hard day at work. They have struggled under pressure from bosses and customers all day, and they need to relax. The last thing they want is to have to pour additional emotional and mental energy into a young person who is trying to figure out the most monumental issues of life—but doesn't know how to talk about it in a calm, rational way! Many parents attempt to substitute other things for their time: money, the keys to the car, or the remote to the television. The parents hope such diversions will make the kids happy, or at least buy some time for the parent to recoup from a difficult day.

A lot of parents operate by the "squeaky wheel method": Whoever is calling most loudly for attention gets their time and energy. Yet if other unseen and unheard struggles are ignored too long, sometimes it becomes too late to effect positive change that could have been done so easily before the problem escalated. Lack of parental attention and love (or even the perceived lack) adds to the stress level of developing young people, which makes them more needy and vulnerable. In response, parents feel even more overwhelmed by these growing needs, and the cycle continues.

Young people today are growing up in an incredibly affluent time. Even with occasional economic downturns, today's families have more disposable wealth than any previous generation. And the children are racking up!

Even young people from relatively modest homes have far more material possessions than the rich kids of a generation ago. I've talked to some kids who, when they are asked what they want for Christmas, just shrug because they already have everything they can imagine. Yet video games, cars, clothes, and all the other trappings of wealth are a very poor substitute for the love and attention the young people desperately need.

IN THE EYES OF GRANDPARENTS

Everywhere I go, I talk to older adults who tell me how much they want to help their grandchildren. I sense the intensity of their commitment in the tone of their voices, the look in their eyes, and their willingness to devote time and resources to their family members. One lady wanted advice about how to put money away for her grandson's college education. (She didn't exactly say it, but I don't think she trusted her daughter to manage the money she wanted to give for the young man's education.) This dear lady told me that she didn't have the opportunity to go to college, but she wanted her grandson to have every advantage toward future happiness and success.

Many grandparents volunteer their time where their grandchildren go to school so they can have a presence and an impact not only on their own grandkids, but also on many other children. They want to make sure the school gets the benefit of their time and energies so these dear children receive the best education they can get.

Some grandparents have witnessed the pain in the lives of their children and their grandchildren caused by divorce, addictions, deaths, or the consequences of bad decisions. They have gone to pastors or counselors to ask for wisdom about how to make a difference. Sometimes their involvement is wanted; sometimes it's not, at least not by one or more in the equation. It takes genuine wisdom to know what to do and how to do it, and these grandparents know they need additional insight to keep from making matters worse, even as a result of their good intentions.

Some grandparents express grief and guilt over their own shortcomings as parents. As they see their own errors replicated in the parenting of another generation, they want to right the wrongs of the past as much as they can. One man told me, "I've apologized to my son for not being there with him as much as I should have been, but the damage is done. Now I see him making the same mistake with his two children, and it breaks my heart. I'm trying to step in and be there for them . . . in a way I wasn't there for my son."

> *Some grandparents express grief and guilt over their own shortcomings as parents.*

Time after time, in conversation after conversation, I've seen deep desire and hope in the eyes of grandparents who want to make a difference in their grandchildren's lives. But I've also noticed that the more grandchildren they have, the less they tend to get involved. Older adults with numerous grandchildren simply feel overwhelmed by the sheer volume of need, and they are paralyzed by the fear of someone accusing them of giving attention to one and not to another. In my observations, the grandparents who are most active in the lives of their progeny are those who have six or fewer grandchildren. Those with more are forced to make some choices about how they invest their energies. They can show all of them love, but they can't be intimately involved in dozens of lives. Their challenge, then, is to be creative in finding ways to connect with all of their grandchildren.

Art Linkletter has nine grandchildren and 16 great-grandchildren spread all over the country. He loves them all, but cannot maintain regular contact with some of them. To remedy this problem, he rents a vacation house for a week each year and invites all the kids, grandchildren, and great-grandchildren to come for seven days of fun, laughter, and tears. Large numbers and great distances are overcome by creative solutions like this. Not everybody can pay for the entire family to come to a vacation house for a week, but other creative solutions are available for finding ways to connect with those we love.

Sometimes people ask me, "Can grandparents really make a difference?" My answer is: Absolutely! Children today are looking for sincerity. They are regularly exposed to hype and phony behavior on television, at school, and sadly, in many of their homes. They are looking for, in fact, they are *desperate* for authentic love. That's what grandparents can give them. Kids see through all the marketing efforts to sell them $70 jeans and $100 shoes. When they see the real thing—the warmth of their grandparents' love—they zero in on it like a radar beam.

Grandparents who get involved out of obligation may not get very far in making meaningful connections with young people. Duty is a poor substitute for real love. But if the kids sense that their grandparents truly care for and are excited about them, they will soak up that affection—and it will change their lives. Effective grandparents don't have to be rich, and they don't have to be well-educated. They don't have to win their grandchildren's love with trips to Disney World. They just need to love them. It is the grandparents' authenticity that touches the hearts of kids, not money, college degrees, or prestige in the community.

QUESTIONS GRANDPARENTS ASK

Getting involved across generations is not always easy. As I've talked to grandparents, they've asked me some excellent questions, such as:

- "What can I do? I live a thousand miles away."
- "I don't even get along with my son. How can I win the right to be involved with my grandchildren?"
- "My grandchildren don't respect me. They see me as ancient and irrelevant. How can I get to know them?"
- "I have to be honest: I don't understand them. I don't like their styles and I don't like their music. How can we have a relationship if I'm repelled by them?"

"I don't even get along with my son. How can I win the right to be involved with my grandchildren?"

- "How can I help? Their problems are just too big for me."
- "I can't compete with the other grandparents who have more time and resources. How can I still nurture this relationship with my grandchildren?"
- "I just don't have enough money to make a difference. What can I do?"
- "My grandchildren and I live in two different worlds. They are so much smarter and they have so many more gadgets. Do I have to learn to use the Internet before I can communicate with them?"
- "Where is the line where I need to stop helping? The more I help my grandson, the more it seems like my daughter wants me to be his mother instead of his grandmother."
- "My granddaughter is doing all kinds of strange, self-destructive things. How can I help her and show her I care? After all, I'm not a psychologist."
- "When I get close to my grandson, he pulls away. What's the problem? Am I doing something wrong? Should I just leave him alone and let him work things out on his own?"
- "I want my grandchildren to know the Lord and love Him, but they don't seem too interested. What can I do?"

These are just a few of the questions I hear people asking, and they are just a few of the topics I want to address in this book. Intergenerational relationships have been a source of strength for families in almost every culture throughout history. Today, however, divorce, mobility, and the hectic pace of life have fragmented families, especially along generational lines. Some grandparents feel remote and unwanted; others are expected to take the parents' role in raising the kids. Older adults need guidelines to know how far to go to build hope and strength without taking on responsibilities they shouldn't assume. Most of us need to take initiative to help, but a few of us need to back off and let the parents be parents. There are principles to guide us, but no strict formulas and no simple solutions. The answers to these dilemmas are as varied as the families themselves.

Sometimes family relationships can become strained simply because we make assumptions instead of finding out what other people want. And assumptions, as we all know, can get us into trouble.

When my wife Debbie had our older daughter, Maegan, we made the assumption that my parents would keep her whenever we wanted to go somewhere. My parents were nearby, they were available, and they had always offered to help in any way they could. If we had a meeting or a party, I'd call and inform my Mom and Dad, "We're bringing Maegan over at 6:30 Friday night." I didn't ask; I assumed. And we left Maegan at their house time after time, whenever it was convenient—for us. My parents never complained. They never said, "Well, you could at least ask instead of just telling us!" But after a while (too long, to be honest), Debbie and I realized that assuming they would keep Maegan just wasn't thoughtful. From that day on, we started asking.

PAPAW CROSS

Both of my grandfathers died before I was born. My father was only 16 when his dad died. My mother's father died six years before I was born, when my mother was still young. But by the time I came along, my father's mom had remarried a man, John Henry Cross, who became a dear grandfather to me. In fact, as a child I wasn't aware that Papaw Cross wasn't actually a blood relative. He called all of my grandmother's grandchildren his own, and my grandmother called all of his grandchildren her own. Love does, indeed, cover a multitude of hurts, sins, and anything else that threatens to wreck a family.

All of us realized something very important in our relationship with Papaw Cross: If we gave him something, he genuinely appreciated it. The gift may have been a Christmas present or just something we gave him because we were thinking of him on a spring day. It may have been something expensive, but more often, it was just an inexpensive trinket from a loving child. It didn't matter to him. He treasured everything he was given, and he told everybody who would listen about the wonderful gift (wonderful to him, anyway) that he had received from one of us.

One Christmas when I was a boy, my mother went with me to buy him a shoeshine kit. He was thrilled when he opened it, and a day or so later, he inscribed the top of the box with a cross and both of our initials: "JC" and "PW." It certainly wasn't the finest shoeshine kit in the world, but it was important to him simply because it came from one of his grandchildren. He wanted everybody to know he was proud to have received that shoeshine kit from me. In the years since Papaw Cross died, my grandmother has given back many of the things we gave him. She had no problem knowing who gave each gift because he made careful notes of his appreciation of each one. Today, that shoeshine kit I gave him sits in our home with the hand-made shoetrees he carved. The shoeshine kit is a lasting legacy of a grateful and loving grandfather.

The shoeshine kit is a lasting legacy of a grateful and loving grandfather.

We also got back a Bible we gave him for one of his birthdays. He treasured it, and he knew we would treasure it, too. He saw the Bible and all the other gifts as symbols of our love for him, and now they are symbols of his love for us.

Papaw Cross noticed and affirmed the abilities of each grandchild. He was a student of each of us. He noticed that I asked a lot of questions and I was fascinated with seemingly trivial things. He was a farmer, and late one afternoon, we sat on the porch of his house while I asked him how to plant corn and how much fertilizer it took to make it grow. I asked him all kinds of things, and he was so happy to tell me everything he knew about growing corn. He told me, "You sure have an inquisitive mind!"

I'm sure I talked a lot back then, and I've always remembered his faith in me. One day he took me aside and told me solemnly, "Phil, someday, you are going to do well as a speaker—really well! You've got it in you." (Other grandparents might have told me to just "Shut up!")

Papaw Cross demonstrated his love in so many ways. I felt valued as a person when he spent time talking, explaining, listening, and affirming me. He died when I was very young. To this day, my grandmother talks about how much he treasured his grandchildren.

When I was a growing boy, I had to come to grips with the fact that I wasn't going to be a star athlete . . . or even a moderately good one. That reality can be devastating for a boy from a small town where sports are often the measure of one's worth. During that time, Papaw Cross communicated unconditional acceptance, affection, and affirmation that washed away any sense of self-doubt at not being a gifted athlete. I had some cousins who were very good athletes, but I never remember a single time that he compared me to them. In fact, I don't even remember a single time that he even talked about sports with me at all. If it wasn't important to me, it wasn't important to him.

MY HOPE FOR YOU

It is my heart-felt hope that every child can experience the kind of relationship with a grandparent that I had with Papaw Cross. I wish every child could feel the touch of warmth and see the genuine look of love that I saw. I wish every child could hear the same patient explanations—and not be compared to other kids. I wish every child could feel from time to time like he or she is the most special person in the world, if only for a few

I wish every child could feel the touch of warmth and see the genuine look of love that I saw.

minutes. That's the gift Rachel gave Suzanne, and it's the gift Papaw Cross gave me.

My relationships with my grandmothers, which I'll describe later in the book, were just as positive as the one I enjoyed with Papaw Cross. Although those two women were nothing at all alike, they both gave me love, attention, and direction.

My grandparents were not rich. They didn't win my love by giving me expensive gifts. In fact, a typical Christmas present was a pair of socks. But they gave me something far more valuable than any tangible possession. They gave me love and time.

The principles in this book will help you make a difference in the life of your grandchild. Perhaps that child is doing fine, and you simply want to encourage him or her the way Papaw Cross encouraged me. But maybe the grandchild is hurting and acting out in destructive ways. Perhaps your heart breaks because you want so much to help. If so, your heartbreak is a wonderful sign of authentic compassion. It's people like you who care enough to jump into difficult situations, to put your arm around someone who, perhaps, no one else is able to get close to. God may use your affection, your attention, and your pointed affirmation to turn a young life around. Years from now, won't it be wonderful if your grandchild talks about you in the same way I talk about Papaw Cross?

But there's another benefit in being grandparents who care enough to get involved: The process will change us, too. If we care, we must trust God for wisdom so we will know how to help most effectively. If we care, we will often have to travel the difficult path between the hurting grandchild and the parents who, for whatever reason, aren't providing the love that child needs. And if we care, we will gladly spend our money, our time, and our energies for the welfare of the grandchild.

As we take action to care, we will be changed. We will grow wiser because we have gained understanding. We will grow emotionally stronger because we have made hard decisions. We will become more tenderhearted as we give and receive love. And we will become more optimistic as we cling to the hope that, even in seemingly hopeless situations, God is at work.

Reading books is of great value to stimulate thinking and teach us principles, but I've found that pointed questions and exercises help me apply those principles more specifically to my own life. Perhaps you will too. At the end of each chapter, you'll find a reflection section. Take time to think, pray, and consider how the content of each chapter can shape your attitudes and actions so you will become a more positive factor in your grandchild's life.

REFLECTION

1. What needs are clearly evident in the lives of each of
    your grandchildren?

2. What do you suspect are unseen needs of each
    grandchild, based on signs you have noticed?

3. List each of your grandchildren and their ages. Next to each one, describe what children of that age typically are learning about life. (For instance, little children are learning basic motor skills and communication. Grade school children are developing analytical and social skills. Adolescents are wrestling with life's basic questions: Who am I? Where do I belong? What can I contribute?)

4. Describe your relationship with each of your grandparents.

5. How did each of your grandparents shape your life in positive ways?

6. What, if anything, do you feel was missing from your relationships with your grandparents?

7. What is your hope for your grandchildren, and specifically, the one(s) who prompted you to read this book?

8. Describe the kind of relationship that you want to create and nurture with those specific grandchildren.

CHAPTER 2

What Makes 'Em Tick

❦

"For the times they are a-changin'."
—Bob Dylan

B ob Dylan wrote "The Times They Are A-Changin' " in 1963 at the dawn of the Civil Rights Movement. It was a time of social upheaval in America, but the song's message applies to the shift from any generation to the next. And if you can remember when the song first hit the charts, you know how much things have changed since then!

To track and compare trends in our culture, we often use the term "generations." Each generation is characterized by its own set of values and behaviors, and each one relates to those before it in particular ways, usually to the dismay of those in the previous generation.

The very concept of "teenagers" is a relatively recent phenomenon in history. For thousands of years, young people were thought to be children until they became adults. As soon as they could work in the fields or the factories, children passed immediately into the world of adult responsibilities. The Jewish bar mitzvah ceremony recognizes this rite of passage from boys to men at the age of 13.

Sociologists disagree about the first recorded mention of the term "teenager," but it wasn't widely used until after World War II. In his book, *Saving the Millennial Generation,* Dawson McAllister observed, "The concept of a leisured youth took hold after World War II, and the term *teenagers* became part of the popular vocabulary around the same time. Teenagers became an identifiable group of people, and they basked in the newfound wealth and attention of postwar America. The prosperity of the '50s coincided with strong families, community friendliness, and rapid suburban growth. Television shows that represent this generation of families include *Leave It to Beaver* and *Father Knows Best.*"[1] After the war, the new subculture of teenagers developed its own language, customs, clothes, and music. In only a few short years, adolescence became a new class in our society, and a new market for consumer goods.

To understand what makes young people tick, we need to look at how their values and behaviors have been shaped.

GENERATIONS

To understand what makes young people tick, we need to look at how their values and behaviors have been shaped. And to understand our own reactions to

---

1 Dawson McAllister, *Saving the Millennial Generation,* (Thomas Nelson, Nashville, Tennessee, 1999), p. 3.

today's youth, we need to take a good, hard look at the forces that have shaped our values and behaviors.

We can identify several specific generations in the past 75 years or so:

- Seniors, born before 1927 (the older part of "The Greatest Generation," popularized by Tom Brokaw's books);
- Builders, born between 1927 and 1945 (younger men and women in "The Greatest Generation");
- Baby Boomers, born between 1946 and 1964 (named because of the post-war boom in births);
- Baby Busters, born between 1965 and 1983 (named because of the rare decline in the birthrate after the postwar boom years), also known as "Generation X"; and
- Millennials, born between 1984 and 2002 (named because they were born on or near the turn of the Millennium), also known as "Generation Y" or "Mosaics."[2]

The middle years in each of these time periods offer the clearest pictures of the generational trends. The closer we get to the transition to the next generation, the more blurred the distinctions become. For example, someone born in 1982 may have as much in common with Busters as Millennials.

George Barna calls today's young people "Mosaics" because their values aren't formed around a single,

---

2 For more on generations, see *The Fourth Turning* by William Strauss and Neil Howe, *Generating Hope* by Jimmy Long, *Women Reaching Women* by Chris Adams, and *Saving the Millennial Generation* by Dawson McAllister.

distinct concept. Instead, they patch together a wide range of seemingly disconnected and often conflicting values in forming their identities. Barna notes of the current generation of young people:

- "their lifestyles are an eclectic combination of traditional and alternative activities;
- they are the first generation among whom a majority will exhibit a nonlinear style of thinking—a mosaic, connect-the-dots-however-you-choose approach;
- their relationships are much more racially integrated and fluid than any we have seen in U.S. history;
- their core values are the result of a cut-and-paste mosaic of feelings, facts, principles, experiences and lessons;
- their primary source of information and connection—the Internet—is the most bizarre, inclusive, and ever-changing pastiche of information ever relied upon by humankind; and
- the central spiritual tenets that provide substance to their faith are a customized blend of multiple-faith views and religious practices."[3]

Their core values are the result of a cut-and-paste mosaic of feelings, facts, principles, experiences and lessons.

---

3 George Barna, *Real Teens,* (Regal, Ventura, California, 2001), p. 17.

With all the significant changes from generation to generation, it's not surprising that the lament I hear over and over is, "I just don't understand my grandchild!" Today's young people are unlike any other generation. Their behaviors seem so strange, and their reasoning is, well, beyond reason. How did they get to this point? What factors have shaped their lives to make them so difficult for grandparents to understand? Some insights to these questions can be found by tracking the trends of the past three generations. The average age of childbirth has remained near 24 years old, so for the sake of comparing generations, we will look at events, media, and cultural trends from 1955, 1979, and today.

Women's clothes

In 1955, cotton was king, but synthetics were coming on the market. Women still spent hours each week ironing. Poodle skirts and bobby socks were the rage for young women. The visible calf was fashionable.

In 1979, synthetics had conquered the fashion scene. Convenience was the top priority. The popularity of miniskirts had come and gone. Bras were out. Lots of leg could be clearly seen—and more was suggested.

Today we find both high fashion and grunge in the same mall and on the same sidewalk. Young women seem to have a compulsion to show their bellybuttons everywhere they go, and those bellybuttons often have something stuck in them! Fashion leaves little to the imagination when it comes to many body parts.

Hairstyles

1955 styles were often short and curled. "Alabama cheerleader" beehives would come a few years later.

Some women still wore their hair long and curly in 1979, but many cut it short and cute.

Today women spend a bundle of money to make their hair look as carefree as possible, and they use color like it is shampoo.

Food preparation

Women slaved in the kitchen for hours most days in 1955 to serve "three square meals" to their busy families. The advances they appreciated were in larger, better refrigerators and stoves.

Tupperware became the rage in the 70s, and the convenience-conscious women of 1979 used anything and everything to save time for other things. Carryout pizza had taken hold as a staple of American cuisine.

Today, we have become polarized between those who live on fast-food and those who are health-conscious, and never the two shall meet—except in passing in the grocery stores!

Communications

In 1955, those who wanted to talk to a friend usually walked next door or wrote a letter. Phone calls were certainly an option, but long distance was expensive.

By 1979, mobility had moved friends and family across the city or across the country. We burned up the phones calling each other.

Today, cell phones, email, and instant messaging have transformed communications.

Television

Television history was made when Lucille Ball was depicted as the first pregnant woman on the small screen in *I Love Lucy*. *Peter Pan* won the Emmy for Best Program for 1955, and Mary Martin won Best Actress for the lead role. Ed Sullivan had the Best Variety Series, and *Your Hit Parade* was the Best Music Series winner.

In 1979, *Lou Grant* and *MASH* swept the Emmys.

Today, political intrigue of *The West Wing*, Mafia brutality of *The Sopranos*, and blatant sexuality of *Sex and the City* dominate television. One of the most popular comedies over the last decade is the animated show, *The Simpsons*, which parodies everything Boomers hold dear. The show, its producer declared in a recent interview, is designed "to encourage the anarchist in all of us."

Movies

Marty won the Oscar in 1955 for Best Picture, and Ernest Borgnine won Best Actor for his role in that film. Anna Magnani (remember her?) won Best Actress for *The Rose Tattoo*.

In 1979, Dustin Hoffman won Best Actor for *Kramer vs. Kramer*, which also won Best Picture. The film depicts the torment of a family ripped apart by divorce, which had become a cultural reality in about half the homes in America. The *Star Wars* trilogy had become widely popular among youth culture.

Today, big-budget films with dazzling special effects are the box office favorites. Tolkien's trilogy, *Lord of the Rings*, is rivaled by a host of eye-popping movies, including the newest *Star Wars* films, for special effects wizardry.

Music

Songs from the mid-50s sound tame by today's standards. Top songs from 1955 included "The Yellow Rose of Texas," "Cry Me a River," and "Unchained Melody."

What a difference a generation makes! By 1979, popular music had been transformed! Elvis, Woodstock, and the Beatles had already come and gone. Acid rock and psychedelic music developed as a part of the new drug culture, before going underground. The Grammy for Best Record of the Year went to the Doobie Brothers for *What a Fool Believes*, and Album of the Year, *52nd Street*, went to Billy Joel.

Today the music scene is dominated by "boy bands" (like 'N Sync and The Backstreet Boys) and the voices and navels of Britney Spears and Christina Aguilera. Hip-hop has grown beyond its urban African-American roots to become a national phenomenon—much to the dismay of grandparents and others who were just getting used to Barry Manilow and James Taylor!

Computers

In 1955, only a handful of people in the world knew about UNIVAC, the computer created by Remington Rand. The Model 409 was the first electromagnetic computer of modular design.

By 1979, mainframe computers were becoming popular in large businesses and in government. Apple had been marketing its version of a personal computer for two years; IBM's first PC was still two years away. The concept of the Internet had been proposed in 1974, and Bill Gates had founded Microsoft four years earlier.

Today, technology is advancing at a staggering pace. We are not only wired; we are now wireless. Business productivity is based on instant access of information and communication. Email has become the preferred choice for communicating, surpassing phone calls and (now ancient history) personal letters.

Exposure to sexually explicit material

In the mid-50s, the raciest material available to most young people was photographs of naked natives in *National Geographic.*

By 1979, *Playboy* and a host of other pornographic magazines were available at virtually every newsstand.

Today, the Internet makes pornography, in numerous deviant forms, readily available to anyone who has access—child or adult.

Average income
     1955—$4137.
     1979—$17,533.
     2002—$38,500.

Average new car prices
     1955—$1910.
     1979—$5758.
     2002—$21,000.

Average price of a new house
     1955—$10,950.
     1979—$58,099.
     2002—$149,165.

Cost of a loaf of bread
1955—18 cents.
1979—47 cents.
2002—$1.99.

Headline news stories

In 1955, the Soviet Union detonated an H-bomb. Disneyland opened in Anaheim, California. Adolph Coors experimented with aluminum beer cans to replace bottles. James Dean died in a car wreck.

In 1979, the Three Mile Island accident was the worst nuclear incident in American history. The Shah of Iran was deposed, and U.S. Embassy personnel were taken hostage. The Soviet Union invaded Afghanistan, and President Jimmy Carter arranged a peace treaty between Egypt and Israel.

Today, the world still reels from the September 11, 2001, terrorist assault on the World Trade Center and the Pentagon. The War on Terrorism continues, shaping our foreign and domestic agendas. Tensions in the Middle East continue to rise.

ADDITIONAL FACTORS

A quick examination of the previous trends gives us an interesting, and often amusing, picture of the vastly different experiences in the lives of grandparents, parents, and children, but other phenomena are even more significant in shaping various generations. The cultural revolution of the late 60s and 70s saw young people throw off the constraints of their parents to indulge in drugs, sex, and alternative lifestyles. Once they lost the glue of the sanctity of marriage, divorce became an easy way out of difficult relationships. The fragmentation of the family was accompanied by increased mobility, so family members and friends were often separated by hundreds or thousands of miles.

Baby Busters who grew up in homes affected by these fractured, distant relationships became cynical and suspicious. Many cultural analysts predicted that the children of Busters, the Millennials, would become even more negative and pessimistic than their parents, but those prophets seem to be wrong.

Many cultural analysts predicted that the children of Busters, the Millennials, would become even more negative and pessimistic than their parents, but those prophets seem to be wrong.

A surprising trend

In spite of the cynicism of their parents, today's young people are surprisingly positive in their attitudes about the present and the future.[4] In contrast to the Busters' pessimism about ever having a meaningful career, today's young people are determined to find meaning and purpose in their work. They believe they can achieve. To facilitate this goal, Millennials see their education as essential preparation, not just "something to do" or a concession to placate their parents.

Young people today are also very interested in spirituality, but not necessarily traditional forms of worship.

---

4 Adapted from Barna, *Real Teens*, p. 23.

Busters, buffeted by painful experiences of abandonment brought on by their parents' divorces, developed fragile egos and tend to take themselves very seriously, but Millennials are more stable and secure, and they relate to others more comfortably.

Stages of development

Normal changes in human development are inextricably woven into the mix of the cultural changes in generations. These changes add yet another layer of complexity to our understanding of today's young people.

Psychologist Erik Erikson and other observers have noted that people go through distinct stages of development. The first several stages are less influenced by culture. They include: the development of trust as an infant depends on parents for sustenance and protection; a growing autonomy as the child takes initiative to walk, talk, use the toilet, and play with toys; the early stages of the development of social skills as the child interacts with other children; and a sense of competence as the elementary and middle school child acquires skills to study, communicate clearly, and produce things on his own.

The adolescent child enters a stage of development which, Erikson taught, is the most critical one in the entire process. During the years of adolescence, the child asks the questions, "Who am I?" "Why am I here?" and "Where do I belong?" Solving this identity crisis requires using the skills learned in the earlier stages: trust, independence, and competence. A child in this stage compares himself to others around him to determine what is acceptable and unacceptable. At this crucial juncture, the messages of culture shout loudly to shape the person's identity, values, and behaviors for the rest of his life.

Young people are sponges. They soak up what is around them. In the early stages, they soak up the attitudes and confidence levels provided by their family environment. In adolescence, however, the culture becomes the ocean in which the sponge floats.

The impact of music

Every culture has distinctive music, and the post-World-War-II generations are no exception. At the close of the war, Frank Sinatra was the biggest star among the women whose boyfriends had gone to war. His hits were still traditional love songs and ballads, but his style was appealing to a younger audience. As the teenage culture developed throughout the next decade, a new sound, one that appealed exclusively to that subculture, began to emerge. Buddy Holly and Chubby Checker built momentum in music for teenagers that Elvis and the Beatles continued and made wildly popular.

Music plays a vital role in shaping the attitudes of young people. That has been true for generations, and because of the availability and proliferation of music, it is a factor today more than ever. Everywhere we go, we see young people plugged in. They wear headsets to listen to CD players in their hip pockets; they listen to music in their cars (with the bass cranked up so much it shakes the cars *next* to theirs); they listen when they study, when they work, when they're together, and when they're alone. Music is the air they breathe. Like every generation—including yours!—their music is offensive to their elders. In fact, if it's not offensive, it's not cool.

Journalist John Weir studied the new hip-hop phenomenon of morphing sounds into heavy beat dance music, and he concluded, "Every generation needs a private language that people over 30 can't translate." That statement may or may not have been true before Elvis and the Beatles, but it certainly has been true since they led the music revolution in the late 50s and 60s. So if you don't understand their music, that's the point. They don't *want* you to. They want something that's exclusively theirs. If you like it, they'll keep looking until they find something you can't stand!

> *"Every generation needs a private language that people over 30 can't translate."*

When you turn on an "oldies" station today and listen to the Beach Boys, the Platters, or the Monkees, those songs bring back memories, don't they? But think back to when they were first hits. If your parents were like countless other adults at the time, they hated those songs! And that just made you and your friends more excited about listening to the forbidden beat.

Diversity and tolerance

For those of us who grew up before the Civil Rights Movement, segregation was a simple and stark reality. One friend remembers, "I didn't have a single friend outside my own race. It wasn't that I was a racist. It simply never occurred to me to have black or Hispanic or Asian friends." But times have changed. The upheaval of the Civil Rights Movement and the subsequent diversity in our culture has made race far less an issue to young people today, especially those who live in cities.

A Caucasian father of a university student told me, "My daughter has more Asian friends than white friends. I think that's great, but my grandmother would roll over in her grave if she knew it!" The issue of race in our culture has moved from the acceptance of segregation, to the uncomfortable confrontations during the 60s, to gradual integration, and now to the acceptance of diversity. Some who are reading this are thinking, "Well, not in my house!" That may be true, but your house is not where the culture is being shaped. College campuses, legislatures, and the media are the proving grounds for testing new ideas and making them a reality in our land. Most grandparents had no close friends from another race; most parents may have had one or two; but the vast majority of young people today have several friends who are of a different race or ethnicity.

Tolerance is among the top values in the culture of the young today. The chief sin today is not drug abuse or murder or robbery. The worst thing that can be said about someone is to call him or her "judgmental." Youth speaker Dawson McAllister has observed that young people "are passionately tolerant, that is, totally intolerant of anybody who takes sides or says something is right or wrong. For those of us who are Boomers, and even for some who are [Busters], the lack of absolutes is baffling. It's easy to lose patience with kids who are adamant only about the absence of anything to be adamant about."[5]

Experience over reason

Grandparents who read this book can point to a few fundamental lessons they learned growing up, and surely one of those was, "Think before you act." Today, however, thinking and reasoning take a back seat to experience. The measure of reality is a person's experience, not what a book or a religion or another person says it is. Relativism has been eating away at the foundation of truth for many years. We can go as far back as the Age of the Enlightenment for the first cracks in the foundation, but the gap has certainly widened at an alarming rate in recent years.

In 1987, Allan Bloom wrote *The Closing of the American Mind,* the first major work about the impact of relativism in our culture. Bloom showed how it has affected learning processes in public schools and universities. George Barna has also chronicled this slide from truth, publishing the findings of his research in books like *The Frog in the Kettle, The Invisible Generation,* and *Baby Busters: The Disillusioned Generation.* Christian writer, speaker, and apologist Josh McDowell used Barna's research in his ground-breaking book about students' valuing experience over reason in *Right from Wrong.*

Among young people today, a common argument is: "That may be true for you, but it's not true for me. Our truths are different." It's hard to reason with someone who is completely comfortable with multiple

---

5 McAllister, *Saving the Millennial Generation,* p. 91.

versions of truth, with his own version that is perfectly suitable and rational to him. The erosion of truth is a fundamental problem in communicating with young people today.

There is nothing right or wrong about, say, the choice between pepperoni pizza and Italian sausage pizza (though I prefer Italian sausage). In that case, personal preference is the determining factor. But in matters of conscience and values, of right and wrong, more is involved

It's hard to reason with someone who is completely comfortable with multiple versions of truth, with his own version that is perfectly suitable and rational to him.

than personal preference. Relativism undermines the thinking process and leaves people with their own feelings as a shaky foundation for determining their choices. Grandparents need to understand that the thought processes of their grandchildren are not logic-based, but experience-based. That is a fundamental difference in the generations.

Energy and creativity

Perhaps in reaction to the Busters' cynicism, Millennials are very active and creative when it comes to solving problems. Order may have been a high virtue for Boomers and their parents, but today's young people despise routine. Their lives are filled with sound bytes, video clips, instant messages, emails, and cell phone calls. A hundred years ago, the average person saw and heard about 100 messages a day; today, we are bombarded with about 30,000. The mass of messages may have numbed the Busters, but it energizes their children! The Millennials accept all the changes and thrive on them. They refuse to be pinned down by a certain schedule. They want to be free to determine what they do and when they do it. If it's important enough, they insist, they'll get to it—eventually.

With so many possible connections provided by the Internet and cell phones, Millennials understandably could feel overwhelmed and withdraw into a shell. But they haven't. They invest their energy into a niche group (a club, youth group, team, etc.), and build relationships there.

Optimism

Only a few short years ago, cultural analysts anticipated the Millennials would be even more brittle, withdrawn, and negative than their Buster parents. The theory was that the models set by isolated, angry victims of divorce couldn't produce anything but more pessimistic children. But Barna's recent research shows a striking—and very encouraging—trend: Millennials are hopeful and optimistic.

Their grandparents marched in Viet Nam or the Civil Rights Movement, and their parents buckled under the traumas of divorce and an increasingly mobile culture. Yet Barna's research shows that the majority of Millennials are optimistic about the future (four out of five), think of themselves as physically attractive (three out of four), and are happy (nine out of ten). Most of them consider themselves leaders, popular with their peers, and having solid, trusting relationships with others. Only a third say they are "stressed out," and only a tenth say they are lonely.

The independent lifestyle of these young people may have led to their self-reliance, competence, and confidence. They are mobile and know how to get around on their own. They are skilled communicators who are connected at several different levels through personal interaction and technology. Nine out of ten feel self-sufficient and responsible, and almost as many are confident enough to describe themselves as "very intelligent." Barna concludes that the prophets of doom were wrong about this generation: "These are not the views of a dour, downcast group with little hope for the future."[6]

THE MOSAIC OF MEANING

Young people today feel completely comfortable with complexity, unafraid of uncertainty, and at home on the road. Their thoughts and beliefs are, indeed, a mosaic of meaning. Millennials are confident in themselves, but they aren't sure where they are going. They are very serious about spirituality, though they aren't sure what version of "truth" they can count on. They are absolutely committed to meaningful relationships, but almost unlimited mobility means their circle of friends often changes. Much of their music is filled with brutal and sexual messages, but they believe they can have kind, committed

> *Young people today feel completely comfortable with complexity, unafraid of uncertainty, and at home on the road.*

6 Barna, *Real Teens*, p. 46.

relationships. Their preference in television (if they watch at all) is cynical and sensual, but they describe themselves as optimistic and secure. In fashion they are devoted to famous designers, but they are fiercely individualistic.

No wonder it is so hard for Boomers and Busters to understand the current generation!

A chart will help us see the differences in the generations:

Boomers	Busters	Millennials
Conquer	Fragmented	Connected
Get ahead	Get away	Get along
Product	Process	Information
Live to work	Work to live	Live to know
Innovative	Adaptive	Analytical
Job first	Family and friends first	Niche group first
Trust demanded	Trust earned	Trust reborn

Adapted from several sources.

THREE CHOICES

In a Middle East crisis, diplomats who are trying to get two cultures to relate to each other have three options: to condemn, accommodate, or empathize. In relating to your grandchild, you have those same three options. Let's look at them.

Condemn them

When we don't understand people, and especially if their behaviors or attitudes cause us pain, the most natural response is condemn them. We point out the stupidity of what they're doing (in our humble opinion) and tell them (in our infinite wisdom) what they need to do to be a better person. But such a response on our part leads to condemnation.

In some cases, we punish those we don't understand by yelling, slamming doors, and calling names. Why do we condemn people like this? For two reasons: For us, it feels good and right, and for them, we hope it will have an impact and change them. The first reason is selfish, the second is manipulative, and both are wrong.

The goal of any relationship is not for the other person to make us feel better. The goal is to love, encourage, and strengthen the other person. That doesn't mean we can always say pleasant things, but it means that most of what we say is powerfully positive. When we have to say something corrective, we say it very thoughtfully and carefully, and always in the context of a wealth of positive messages.

There are times, to be sure, when we have to "lay down the law" with someone and set clear boundaries of acceptable behavior. Yet the other person can easily distinguish between correction (for his or her own good) and condemnation. The desire to control other people is never motivated by love. Exerting too much control over their lives won't help young people grow up to be responsible and independent.

Exerting too much control over their lives won't help young people grow up to be responsible and independent.

Accommodate them

When we give in to others' demands without speaking the truth, we are accommodating them. Giving in may seem like love, but it isn't. Forfeiting our own integrity for the sake of avoiding conflict is just a different (and easier) method of trying to control the person. Grandparents accommodate grandchildren in various ways: giving them money every time they ask for it, letting them do anything they want, or allowing them to stay out as long as they please and hang around people of questionable character.

Jesus is the ultimate example of showing love to others. His love extended to the whole world. He loved people so much that He laughed with them and spoke the truth to them. He listened long and hard, and He patiently answered questions even when other people didn't understand. Ultimately, He was willing to suffer and die to be sure they—and we—understood the depth of His love.

Jesus said He didn't come to judge the world, even though there was plenty to condemn and judge. Yet He didn't accommodate people either. He never said, "It doesn't matter what you do. It'll be OK with me." It wasn't OK. He called a spade a spade. His love included complete forgiveness of all previous sinful behavior, and it continued with His desire to help us avoid further sinful behavior in the future. Jesus demonstrates that rare combination of genuinely understanding and wanting to help others, yet maintaining one's integrity. That's the definition of empathy.

Empathize with them

Listening—really listening—takes courage and tenacity. When we disagree with what we're hearing, it's easy to jump in with the answer. When we discover a problem, it's easier to fix it than to coach a young person to solve it herself. True empathy means that we do whatever it takes to genuinely understand, but we refuse to give in to easy answers. We never settle for condemnation or accommodation.

If you are reading this book, you are committed to empathy. You have a genuine desire to understand how your grandchild thinks and feels. Yes, times have changed, but that doesn't mean you can't bridge the gaps between you! You are committed to wading through the swamp of different values and behaviors, putting aside the assumptions you have developed, and finding common ground so you can love and be loved, understand and be understood.

> *You have a genuine desire to understand how your grandchild thinks and feels.*

James encourages us to "be swift to hear, slow to speak, slow to wrath" (James 1:19). That's empathy. That's how to pursue a person whose behavior is baffling to you, whose music is offensive, and whose clothes are disgusting. It's how to look beyond those surface things and into the heart, to see what is good and right and beautiful.

Jesus modeled empathy perfectly. John wrote about Him, "For the law was given through Moses, but grace and truth came through Jesus Christ" (John 1:17). Jesus' kindness was not spineless accommodation. He boldly spoke the truth—about God, about the hearts of people, about their actions, and about the importance of values and behavior. He never used truth to bludgeon or condemn people. In fact, He told Nicodemus, "For God did not send His Son into the world to condemn the world, but that the world through Him might be saved" (John 3:17).

As a result, people flocked to Him. Children, who are often surprisingly perceptive about the hidden motives of adults, delighted in His presence. Jesus is our example of incorporating grace and truth in our relationships with our grandchildren. We can learn to look past their questionable fashions to see their hearts. We can learn to listen not to their loud music, but to their inner needs. Then we can love them no matter what. And when we need to speak the truth to them, that truth will be more about the love of God and His goodness than about their behavior. Jesus was willing to correct people, sometimes very bluntly, but His grace was unchanging. May the same be said about us.

> *Grandparents need to realize that their grandchildren may have the same last name and the same bloodline, but they live in a different culture.*

REACHING OUT TO A DIFFERENT CULTURE

It is a fundamental (if completely understandable) error to assume that other people are just like us. Grandparents need to realize that their grandchildren may have the same last name and the same bloodline, but

68

they live in a different culture. If we fail to grasp that fact, it limits our ability to connect with them. We will be confused and frustrated when they don't think, feel, and act the way we do, and they will miss out on the benefits we long to give them.

If you were sent across the globe on a humanitarian mission to take food and clothes to desperately needy people, you would need to understand their culture so your help would be accepted. No matter how strong your love for the people and your desire to help them, you would do little good if you offered hamburgers to a culture where cows are sacred, appliances to those in jungles where electricity isn't known, American Sunday clothes to women in Saudi Arabia, bikinis to Eskimos, or parkas to Hawaiians. The best intentions don't make up for a lack of cultural understanding. These examples seem obvious, but the need to span cultural differences between our grandchildren and ourselves may not be so apparent.

I know of a loving grandmother who wanted to do something very special for her grandson who was in high school. She was a terrific seamstress who made her own beautiful clothes, so she decided to make him a shirt for Christmas. She looked through the catalogs and found just the right pattern. For weeks, she labored in love to make the shirt. It had a wide collar and oversized buttons. The fabric was exactly like what she had seen in the catalog. As Christmas approached, she was excited about giving it to him, and on Christmas morning, she proudly watched as he unwrapped the gift. "You're going to love this!" she told him. "I want you to wear it tomorrow to church." She could hardly wait to see the look on his face!

When the last piece of carefully placed tissue paper was finally removed, the young man's eyes looked like saucers. He was speechless! When he held it up, his sister had to cover her mouth to keep from laughing out loud. After a few seconds of strained silence, she and her brother both exploded in laughter. The shirt, made with the utmost love, was something he wouldn't wear in the dark in his own closet. Though he thanked his grandmother over and over (because he knew she had spent lots of time and lots of love on this gift), his words couldn't cover up the truth. The gift was a bomb! His grandmother was devastated. A decade later, that shirt is still neatly folded in the bottom of his drawer at his parents' home. He occasionally opens that drawer to get something else, sees the shirt, and is reminded of his grandmother's love. But he will never, ever wear that shirt—not in a million years.

This dear grandmother made assumptions that were not at all correct. It would have been much more productive if she had told her grandson, "I want to get you a very nice shirt for Christmas. Would you go to the mall with me so you can pick it out?" They would have had the pleasure of spending time together, and she would have enjoyed seeing him wear it. While her love in making the shirt was never in question, her assumptions were misguided. The labor of love simply didn't connect with her grandson the way she hoped it would.

I'm not saying that you change everything about yourself in order to relate to your grandchildren, but I am suggesting that you understand today's youth culture so you can avoid common mistakes. You may have enjoyed fishing with a cane pole on a bank, but today's high-tech fishing enthusiasts may expect a fast boat with a depth finder and the latest innovations in rods and reels. You may not be able to afford the latest gear—or even want it—but it costs nothing to watch the fishing shows on television and be able to talk about the latest gear and techniques. That will show your grandchildren that you understand, and it will make a world of difference.

Cultural differences create real problems, However, we'll see in the next chapter that when the layers are peeled away, we all need the same things.

REFLECTION

1. What were your favorite television shows in the 50s, 70s, and today?

    Describe the differences in the shows you recall (pace, topic, the depiction of family dynamics, etc.).

2. What was your favorite music when you were young?

How was it different from your parents' music?

How did they react to yours?

3. Before reading this chapter, how would you have described today's youth culture?

Has your opinion changed now that you've read the chapter? If so, explain.

4. What are some reasons we might condemn young people for being different?

What are some reasons we might accommodate them?

What is likely to result in each of these cases?

5. Describe what it means to empathize with young people.

In what way is Jesus an example for you as you relate to younger generations?

CHAPTER 3

Look Beneath the Purple Hair, Tattoos, and Studs

"If there is any one secret of success, it lies in the ability to get the other person's point of view and see things from that person's angle as well as from your own."—Henry Ford

People who know me well know that I am a big fan of the *Andy Griffith Show.* I thoroughly enjoy seeing Andy try to get himself out of the trouble Aunt Bea, Opie, and Barney get him into. In the program titled "The Senior Play," Andy's girlfriend, Helen Crump, is producing the senior class play at the high school where she teaches. Instead of a traditional Shakespearean play, this time the students had chosen a contemporary musical with the rock-and-roll they all loved.

Helen and the kids work on the play for weeks. But when the principal sees a rehearsal, he explodes, "You can't perform this kind of music! Not at my school!" Helen and the kids are devastated, but they don't give up. They rewrite the play to take place in the Roaring Twenties instead of the 60s, with jazz instead of rock-and-roll. They invite the principal back to rehearsal. This time, as he hears the music and sees the costumes familiar to him, he grins and proclaims, "Now, that's music!"

Helen seizes that teachable moment. She explains that the jazz he loved so much when he was young was just as revolutionary—and just as shocking to older adults—as the rock-and-roll her students enjoy. The generation of young people today, Helen reminds him, is not so different from generations past. They all have to carve out their own identities which are distinct and different from their parents.

If we understand that each generation seeks out its own distinctive looks and sounds, we won't be as shocked by our grandchildren's fashions, music, values, and language. And we will be far better prepared to relate to them in meaningful, productive ways.

THE IMPORTANCE OF INSIGHT

The last chapter gave us information and insight about the differences between the generations. In this chapter, we will focus on how we can use that information to build bridges and make a powerfully positive impact on grandchildren.

We pointed out that our natural, human response is to reject anything we don't understand, and we certainly don't understand many of the commercials targeting young people on television. Do we have to look at *another* Britney Spears commercial? Must we hear the blaring rap music with the heavy bass beat? We may be repulsed by such things, yet when we reject their idols and their

When we reject their idols and their sounds, it is a short step for the young people to feel rejected by us as well.

sounds, it is a short step for the young people to feel rejected by us as well.

Older generations have valued clear, cause-and-effect logic. When they saw a need, they took specific action to fix the problem. For example, the Japanese attacked us at Pearl Harbor, so our nation went to war. We were challenged by the Soviets when they put ballistic missiles in Cuba, so President Kennedy imposed an embargo. Today, as we feel threatened by the dramatic decline in morality, we want to enforce steps that will remedy the problem.

We see things on network channels every single night that would have made our parents drop over from shock! Drugs, teen pregnancies, violence, and the host of other problems in today's culture give us ulcers. We see the effects, and we naturally look for causes. The main causes, many of us conclude, are the music and media that entertain and stimulate our young people. The solution: Refuse to let the grandkids get involved in such things. That's it! We've solved the problem.

But all those morality problems aren't going to disappear with a solution that simple. Some of us remember the outcry from the older generations when Elvis was on the *Ed Sullivan Show,* but do we remember how tame his performance actually was? The censors didn't even allow the cameras to show his hips! Today, when we see Britney, Christina, and others on networks or cable shows, little is left to the imagination. We hear today's sitcom characters laughing and talking openly about body parts and the most personal matters. This slide in morality alarms us, and we want it to stop—now!

Our recommendation (and to be honest, often our *demand*) is that our grandchildren stop listening to their music and stop watching the shows that are, in our opinion, contaminating them. Certainly the lyrics and images in the media affect young hearts, but our remedy is one that we wouldn't have been willing to accept from our parents and grandparents when we were young.

NEW EYES TO SEE

Phil Waldrep Ministries hosts a Student Celebration every year after Christmas in Pigeon Forge, Tennessee. A couple of years ago, Josh McDowell spoke at the conference. After one of his talks, he signed books and talked with people until the crowds had thinned. Eight or nine people were still asking him questions when I walked up. About a minute later, Josh leaned over to whisper in my ear: "Don't look too quickly, but I want you to notice the two boys standing in the back of the room."

I had already noticed them. In fact, it was hard not to notice! They had spiked hair, Army boots, baggy pants, tattoos . . . and one had a dog collar around his neck. They looked like they hadn't taken a bath in weeks. "When I finish here," Josh continued to whisper to me, "I want you to go with me to talk to those boys."

After a few more questions and answers, the last person left the book table. Josh nodded for me to follow him, and we walked over to the young men. Josh knew they were waiting to talk, but he didn't begin by asking what they wanted. After exchanging greetings, he said to them, "I want to ask you guys two questions." They smiled and nodded. "The first question is: When do you guys plan to quit school?"

They boys looked at each other and shuffled their feet, then one of them answered, "How did you know we planned to quit school when we went back after Christmas vacation?"

Josh didn't reply. Instead, he asked his second question, "What was your relationship with your Dad like? Tell me about him."

Both young men looked to the floor. One mumbled, "Well, I, uh, don't even know who my old man is."

The other chimed in, "Yeah, me either."

Josh and I talked with these two young men for about an hour and tried to show them genuine compassion without being syrupy. When they walked away from us, both of these seemingly tough, disconnected young men were crying, and they both had made a commitment to Josh to stay in school.

After they walked away, Josh told me, "Their clothes, their hair, and their attitudes scream, 'I'm not going to conform to this culture, because if I do, I'll be rejected—and I can't stand to be rejected again.' These guys stayed in the back of the room while I signed books. They didn't leave because they were hoping somebody—maybe even I—would step into their lives to show them some love. Everything about them is a loud and clear cry for love."

When they walked away from us, both of these seemingly tough, disconnected young men were crying, and they both had made a commitment to Josh to stay in school.

81

He explained what he had seen as he talked to people at the book table. "Those two guys stayed in my view the whole time I was in the back. They weren't going to leave, but they also weren't going to come up to me. If I wanted to talk to them, I had to notice and take the initiative. They were saying, in effect, 'If you care about me, you have to get up from your chair and come into my world. If you don't care, then you won't even notice—or worse, you'll notice and be disgusted and walk away.' " Josh continued, "When we walked over to them, they didn't act defensive at all. In fact, when I asked them the two questions, they answered bluntly and honestly. It would have been easy for them to blow me off and give answers that kept me at a distance, but they spoke the truth. My willingness to get up and go to them disarmed their defenses."

Young people often don't use words to express their wants and needs. In fact, they use forms of communication that seem to say just the opposite of what they really mean. When they color their hair, get tattoos, wear strange clothes, eat too much and become overweight, and do a host of other repulsive things, they aren't really saying, "Stay away from me!" No, they are saying, "If you care enough, you'll look past the repulsive things and step into my life to love me." They are testing us to see if we really care. Will we notice? Will we care enough to get involved? Will we pass the test?

Could Josh have walked away without getting involved with those young men? Of course he could. If you've ever seen Josh speak, you know how much energy he expends. He had answered dozens of questions at the book table and had signed his autograph over and over again. No one would have blamed him at all if he had said, "Hey, I'm tired. I'd love to talk to those guys, but it can wait until tomorrow." But he didn't. He looked beyond their rough exteriors and saw their needs. He looked past their nonverbal message to "Stay away!" and detected their muffled cry for attention and affection.

Grandparents have a unique opportunity to hear a grandchild's pleas for love, direction, and hope—which may be disguised. These are timeless needs, which may be shrouded in repulsive clothing and smells. But if we get beyond the outer facade, we can begin to find fresh ways to communicate our love so those needs are met.

I've discovered that one of the biggest hurdles is that grandparents sometimes feel embarrassed by their grandkids. They see the grandkids' odd behavior and repulsive dress as a reflection of them and their own children, and they can't stand it. They find their own grandchildren revolting, which triggers their embarrassment and anger and short-circuits the love they genuinely want to express.

When it comes to those we love, we have to forget about hair, music, sleazy comedy shows, and all the other things that make us uncomfortable, and we need to see their hearts. We have to be willing to go to the mall with a grandson who wears his jeans so low most of his underwear shows, or go to church with a granddaughter whose eyebrows, tongue, navel, and who-knows-what-else is studded with all kinds of ugly jewelry. Will our friends see us and wag their heads? Yes, they might. Will they whisper and talk about us all

But we have to ask ourselves what is more important: staying in the good graces of some old, grumpy people who talk too much, or showing love to someone whose heart cries out for attention and affection?

over town on the Gossipy Grandparent Hotline? Yes, they probably will. But we have to ask ourselves what is more important: staying in the good graces of some old, grumpy people who talk too much, or showing love to someone whose heart cries out for attention and affection? Your choice.

BE YOUR LOVING SELF

As you try to relate to your grandchild, don't try to be somebody you're not. Don't get your navel pierced and put a boom box on your shoulder to listen to the latest rapper. (There's an image to ponder!) If you try too hard to be "one of them," you'll fail miserably and you'll alienate yourself from your grandchild instead of drawing closer. Remember, kids respond to sincerity and authenticity. Grandma with a navel ring or a grandpa who never misses "Total Request Live" on MTV isn't authentic. Sure, you can ask about the music they enjoy, and their concerts and videos. You need to enter into their world from time to time, but draw the line at showing interest and understanding. Don't try to become one of them.

It's hard to do everything right when attempting to communicate effectively with your grandchildren—especially if you're just getting started. You may make mistakes, and that's OK as long as you learn from them.

I know of a grandmother who was aghast when her grandson bleached his hair white. She told him it was ugly. When that didn't change his mind, she upped the ante by telling him it was morally wrong to color his hair. He didn't let her get away with that. He challenged her, "So it's wrong for me to color my hair?" She nodded. "But Gram, you color your hair at the beauty parlor, don't you?"

She stammered, "Yes. Yes, I do, but that's different."

"How is it different?"

"Well, you dye yours that unnatural white, but I try to keep mine what it used to be."

"So you're saying it's not really a problem about dyeing. It's about the color."

She had to admit that he had her. After some soul searching, she admitted to a friend that she was really reacting to a lot of other things that her grandson enjoyed, especially his choice of music. His hair was just the easiest thing to condemn and try to control. After that day, she never criticized him again for coloring his hair. She had a deeper understanding about herself and him, and she tried to build bridges—instead of blowing up the bridge to her grandson!

Grandparents need to avoid assuming their own grandchildren are involved in the same illegal and immoral actions they see in young people who make the evening news. Fashions and styles don't dictate behaviors. Just because we find out a girl with an eyebrow ring is a prostitute doesn't mean *every* girl with an eyebrow ring is a hooker. Just because a particular boy with baggy pants and spiked hair committed vandalism

while on drugs doesn't mean your junior high grandchild who wears baggy pants and has spiked hair is
doing coke and spray painting graffiti on the side of the
school. A style may or may not indicate something in the
heart. Don't jump to conclusions. Look deeper. False
accusations drive people away like nothing else can.

THE GOAL OF INTERACTION

A grandparent's goal should be to help his or her
grandchildren feel confident and secure. This goal can
be reinforced with every phone call, walk, meal, or any
other means of communicating.

> *A grandparent's goal should be to help his or her grandchildren feel confident and secure.*

Sometimes the young people will be
down and need someone to believe
in them; sometimes they will have
personal achievements to celebrate;
sometimes they feel confused and
need direction; and sometimes they
just need a hug to remember that
someone cares about them.

Countless books have been written about the intrica-
cies and mysteries of human relationships, and indeed,
they can be pretty confusing sometimes! But one simple
and clear principle is the law of sowing and reaping:

- We reap what we sow.
- We reap after we sow.
- We reap more than we sow.

What are you and I sowing in our relationships, especially with grandchildren? A man recently told me, "I
can't remember my grandmother ever saying a kind
word to me, and I can't remember her ever hugging me."

"Did she live far away from you?" I asked.

"No," he responded. "After my grandfather died, she lived in our house."

"Tell me about your relationship," I probed.

"Well, we just kind of coexisted in the same house. She didn't get involved in my life, and I certainly didn't get involved in hers."

This grandmother reaped what she sowed in that relationship. She sowed emotional distance, and that's what she got in return. When this man was a boy, he could have thoroughly enjoyed a warm, loving relationship with his grandmother, and he would have given her a lot of joy and love in return. Maybe she was preoccupied with her own problems. Maybe she had been hurt before and didn't want to risk being hurt again by this grandson. Whatever the cause, her aloofness caused both of them to miss a wonderful opportunity to give and receive love.

In stark contrast, my own relationships with my grandmothers were warm and wonderful. They were excited when they saw me walk through the door or when they heard my voice on the phone, and I was eager to see them every chance I got. They talked to me like I was very important to them, and I soaked up their attention. I guess my responses expressed my love in return, but I never thought about that when I was a child. The shared time, laughter, and affection was the fabric of daily life. I loved it, and they did, too.

Even today, my father's mother is still one of my biggest fans. She has heard me speak a number of times, and she tells everyone who will listen (and maybe a few who don't want to listen!) that, "Phil's the best speaker in America." I know I'm not, but that doesn't matter to her. In her eyes and through her ears, I'm the best.

One thing that assures me how much she values me is that I hear from other people what she has said about me. Third-party comments give us the best indication of what someone really believes. If a girl hears from someone, "Your grandfather is sure proud of you! He can't stop talking about how terrific you are," then she can know he really means it. Somehow, hearing praise from someone else is particularly meaningful.

Of course, the "grapevine" can work to our detriment as well. If someone tells a young person, "I talked to your grandmother the other day and she is really worried about you," that grandchild can be devastated by Grandma's lack of confidence—and her lack of confidentiality. Older people commonly talk to each other and share family concerns, but it is wise for them to be selective about how much to say about their grandchildren—and to whom.

The goal of affirmation is not to get the grandchild to change. That's not love; it's manipulation. The goal of affirming a person is to reinforce his or her sense of identity, to show love, and to build up the person. If others change for the better, that's great, but if not, our affirmation still has great value.

> *The goal of affirmation is not to get the grandchild to change.*

Young people are often very perceptive. Two people can say exactly the same thing. If one says it with the motive of manipulating the child's behavior, those words often will be rejected. But if the grandparent communicates the same message with "non-possessive warmth," that is, with genuine love and without any hint of trying to control the child through affirmation, the grandchild usually soaks up that love.

Affirmation is built upon truth and trust. If you compliment a child in a way that he knows is obviously not true, you may devastate him instead of reinforcing his identity. For example, a grandfather wanted to encourage his clumsy grandson who tried so hard to play basketball, and told him, "You're the best player on the team!" The child knew he wasn't very good—much less the best—so his granddad's words had the opposite impact. They not only discouraged the boy, but also eroded his trust in his grandfather. His grandfather *could* have said, "Son, I'm so proud of you for hustling in practice and being ready whenever the coach wants to put you in. There's not a player out there with more heart than you. That shows real character." Those words would have had the ring of authenticity, and they would be eagerly absorbed by the grandson who so desperately needs genuine affirmation.

CONSISTENCY

Grandchildren look beyond their relationships with us to see what kind of people we are. If they hear us tell the preacher at the front door after church, "Your sermon was very inspiring this morning," and then hear us talk at lunch about how boring he was, our credibility is shattered. The next time they hear a compliment from us, they have every reason to wonder if we really mean what we say. Make no mistake, grandchildren watch us like hawks. If they see us being authentic in what we say to and about others, they will more readily believe we are authentic in what we say to and about them.

Grandkids also watch to see if their grandparents are consistent between what they say and what they do. I know of a ten-year-old boy who got caught for shoplifting at a grocery store. The store manager didn't report the incident to the police, but did tell the boy's father and grandfather, and the boy was disciplined. His grandfather gave him a stern lecture about the importance of being honest. A few weeks later, the grandfather took the boy to the same grocery to buy some milk. While walking through the store, the granddad absent-mindedly picked up a small cluster of grapes and munched on them, then threw away the stem. They got the milk and went to the register to pay for it. The grandchild was watching and listening, but his granddad didn't say a word about the grapes. When they got in the pickup, the boy asked, "Granddaddy, did you steal those grapes?"

The older man shook his head and said, "No, they were probably going to spoil so he wouldn't have sold them anyway."

At the moment the grandfather attempted to justify *his* theft, his previous lecture about shoplifting lost its impact. The granddad's credibility was negated by his behavior, and from then on his moral arguments fell on deaf ears. Consistency is crucial.

Similarly, a grandfather who smokes and drinks has less influence in trying to stop a grandchild from using drugs. A grandmother who is obsessed with her clothes and appearance isn't likely to prevent a granddaughter from spending too much money on the latest styles. Our eating habits, weight, spending, use of time, language, and a host of other behaviors are on display for our grandchildren to see. We don't have to be perfect, but we need to show remorse when we're wrong and be willing to do right when we have the next opportunity.

> *We don't have to be perfect, but we need to show remorse when we're wrong and be willing to do right when we have the next opportunity.*

Some young people have a very clear sense of purpose in their lives, but many wander through adolescence with no clear direction. A certain amount of wandering is a normal part of seeking identity as young people try different things until they find what they like to do and can do it well. But some young people wander too long without finding anything that gives them a benchmark for the future. They drift aimlessly at school, at home, and with friends, with no drive and with little hope for the future.

When we see children who lack purpose, we need to look more deeply than just at their surface behavior. If we peel back a layer or two, we often find that their primary need is for identity and love. Purpose, then, is a function of that identity. A loved, secure person has the emotional strength and the confidence to try new things.

If he succeeds, that's great, and if he fails, it's not the end of the world.

When I was a boy, my family rented a farm from my aunt where my dad raised cattle. In the late afternoon, we'd drive the truck to the barn to make sure they had plenty to eat. The cattle were usually scattered all over the farm, but when they heard that truck, they headed to the barn. Sometimes little calves got left behind and lost when their mothers became preoccupied with their own hunger and moved too quickly toward the food. Today, some kids are like those calves. Their parents and grandparents are preoccupied with their own needs, and the young people are left alone and vulnerable.

One of the most valuable things we can give our grandchildren is the gift of reason. Some grandparents talk easily and often with their grandkids about what happened when they were adolescents and young adults, but few take the time to explain how they learned to make significant choices. The underlying reasons are more important to the grandchild than the choices themselves, and much wisdom can be acquired from digging deeper into the motives and complexities that shaped those decisions.

For example, your grandchild may be well aware that you were a banker or a seamstress or a fireman or a housewife, but may not know the family pressures and the hopes that shaped your decision. He or she will also benefit from hearing how you dealt with the inevitable disappointments you experienced.

I've watched young people who were bored to death hearing (for the 659th time) about the genealogy of a family. But when someone explains that great-grandmother Baker married your great-grandfather because she was afraid no one else would ever ask her, the kids sit up and pay attention. Maybe a teenage girl is afraid she won't have many boys interested in her, and she'll need to say "yes" to the first one who comes along. Hearing about her great-grandmother may give her an opening to talk about her own fears and hopes. In most families, such lessons are almost endless. You can talk about careers and marriages, moves and business decisions, broken relationships and fulfilled dreams, and the good and bad outcomes of many important decisions. Discussing the emotional and relational consequences of your decisions will help guide grandchildren in making the tough choices they face. Children will learn from your successes, but they may learn even more from your struggles and failures. Your honesty makes you a real person to them, and real people are safe people who can be trusted. In a later chapter, we will discuss how to tell your story so that it has the power to change young lives.

Another way grandparents can give direction and hope to their grandkids is for them to be an example of passion and purpose—no matter how old they are. Sadly, many people live for years dreaming of retirement, but discover their lives are empty and barren when that day finally comes. They are drifting just as much as their grandchildren, which isn't a good model for grandchildren to see!

Retirement from one line of work frees us to pursue another goal, sometimes with greater resources and greater passion than we've ever known before. We don't have to be in the best physical condition to have genuine purpose in life. Some elderly people use their time to pray for others, and some help at church, at school, or with Meals on Wheels. My grandmother is 91 years old at this writing, and every day she calls her friends who live alone to check up on them. She's not as mobile as she used to be, but she can dial that phone and see if her friends need anything. That's her purpose, and both she and her friends benefit from her care and efforts. No matter how old or how poor we may be, we have an incredible opportunity to be an example for our grandchildren by showing that we have a clear, driving purpose that gives us a sense of worth and makes a difference in the lives of others.

No matter how old or how poor we may be, we have an incredible opportunity to be an example for our grandchildren by showing that we have a clear, driving purpose that gives us a sense of worth and makes a difference in the lives of others.

Dr. Robert Sittason was my dentist when I was a young man. He is retired now, and he spends his time driving for Meals on Wheels. Not long ago, he sent me a note and said he was having more fun than he ever had in his life! He wrote that he had a wonderful sense of purpose, even more than he had when he was a dentist. Delivering meals to needy people was making a difference in their lives. His children have told me how much they admire their father because he didn't just sit in an easy chair after he retired. He is demonstrating that a person can have a compelling purpose that revs his engines every day, and many people around him—family and friends, young and old—are the beneficiaries of that purpose.

STAGES IN COMMUNICATION

People involved in humanitarian efforts or missions in other cultures often identify three distinct stages in their work. The first stage is the excitement of making contact. Every conversation is fresh and invigorating, and workers experience tremendous hope that they can make a difference. After a few weeks or a few months, however, the drudgery of day-to-day living sets in. The work ceases to be as exciting. The obstacles that seemed insignificant at first begin to nag at their spirit. Misunderstandings arise in their relationships with the people in that other culture. During this stage, many workers want to quit and go home, and some do. But those who stay are forced to dig deeper into their own hearts to find the real motivation for being there. They may have begun because the assignment promised to be fun, but when the initial fun wore off, they had to find a genuine, other-centered love for those in the other culture. This period requires reflection, reassessment, and adjustment—both internally and externally, in their hearts and in their actions.

Those who work through this difficult time and make the necessary shifts in attitude and expectations describe a new depth of communication they never thought possible. The excitement of the first stage and the discouragement of the second are eventually replaced with a deep, lasting joy from showing love day after day, patiently waiting to see positive results.

In the next chapter, we will examine how love and compassion can soothe hurts and give hope to grand-children.

R EFLECTION

1. How do you usually respond to young people like the two boys Josh McDowell noticed in the back of the room?

How do you *want* to respond to such people?

2.   What does it mean to "be your loving self"?

3.   Describe the last three or four interactions you have had with each of your grandchildren.

In each case, what were you sowing in the person's life?

What, then, can you expect to reap?

4. Have you ever seen someone use affirmation to control another person's behavior? If so, describe what happened.

How did that attempt to manipulate control affect the relationship?

5. How would you rate your consistency (between what you say and what you do, and between what you say to your grandchildren and what you say to others)? Why is consistency so important?

6. What are some experiences in your life, painful or pleasant, for which you could explain the underlying reasons for your choices?

How might your grandchild benefit from understanding those reasons?

7.   Describe your own sense of purpose these days.

Do you need to make any changes to "rev your engines"?

8.   Review the three stages of cross-cultural communication. Which stage are you in with each grandchild?

The Compassion Principle: Showing You Care

❦

"Love consists in this, that two solitudes protect and touch and greet each other." —Rainer Maria Rilke

By the time she was 21, Kim had already struggled with drug and alcohol addiction for many years, and was estranged from her parents. One night after getting drunk, she lost control of her car and died as a result of the crash.

After the terribly sad funeral, her parents went to clean out her apartment. At the bottom of Kim's jewelry box, her mother found a crumpled piece of paper. It was a letter Kim's grandmother had written a couple of years before, at the very time Kim's addictions were ruining her relationship with her parents. The letter read:

My dear Kim,

I know you are going through a difficult time, and in many ways, I'm not sure I understand everything that you are thinking and feeling. But I don't have to. I just want you to know that there is nothing you can do that will ever stop me from loving you. No matter where you go, no matter how angry you are at your Mom and Dad—or even me, if that ever happens—I will always cherish you. Whenever you feel alone, I hope you will come to me, call me, or at least think of me. I love you so much. Please don't ever doubt that, and please don't forget that.

Always,
Grandmamma

The letter looked like it had been read dozens of times. It was a treasure to Kim. Perhaps it was wrinkled because she felt so ashamed and anguished when she read it, or perhaps she clenched it in her hand and drew it to her breast when she thought of her grandmother's deep and genuine love. No matter how much pain Kim had caused, and how much suffering she had experienced, she could always come back to this reminder of her of her grandmother's affection.

TAKE THE INITIATIVE

Love doesn't sit idle and watch while people suffer. Love demands that we get involved. It reaches out to touch someone's heart, no matter what he or she has done and no matter what the cost.

It reaches out to touch someone's heart, no matter what he or she has done and no matter what the cost.

In a recent television interview with Bill O'Reilly, actor George Kennedy told a painful story about his family. His daughter and son-in-law had severe drug problems that resulted in the overdose and death of the young man, and a drug possession conviction and prison sentence for Kennedy's daughter. That left their seven-year-old daughter, Taylor, alone. Kennedy explained that he and his wife, at 77 and 70 years old, had taken the responsibility to raise Taylor. They couldn't stand the thought of their granddaughter being sent to a foster home or anywhere else to live with strangers. They changed their schedules, their priorities, and every aspect of their lives to care for this dear girl. O'Reilly asked, "You could have found someone else to take care of her. Why did you take her in?"

Kennedy answered, "We took her into our home because Taylor needs someone whose blood runs through her veins to care for her, tuck her in at night, hug her, and tell her, 'I love you.' "

George Kennedy and his wife certainly had the resources to hire someone to tend to Taylor, but they chose to care for her themselves. No excuses . . . just a commitment to protect that little girl and provide a loving home for her.

BE A STUDENT OF YOUR GRANDCHILD

In his excellent book, *The Five Languages of Love*, Gary Chapman identifies five ways people give and show affection: quality time, words of affirmation, acts of service, physical touch, and giving gifts. Chapman explains that two people may have very different languages of love, so knowing the other person's language is vitally important in order to communicate clearly and effectively. His book is directed to married couples, but the principles apply to grandparents and grandchildren just as well.

For example, a grandmother may delight in showing her love by "giving gifts," such as cooking favorite meals or making new clothes for a grandson. However, if the boy's love language is "quality time," he would much rather sit on the porch and talk or go to the zoo with his grandmother. He wonders why she spends so much time in the kitchen or in front of the sewing machine when he wants to be with her. She is showing love, but he doesn't understand her language.

To communicate well, we need to identify our own love language as well as the language of those we care about. Knowing ourselves is probably pretty easy to accomplish. Just examine what you do at Christmas and birthdays for patterns that reflect your expressions of love. These questions will help you:

- For "quality time": Do you make sure to carve out time to talk to those you love? Do those relaxed or creative times together delight you?
- For "words of encouragement": Do you think about how to say just the right thing to encourage people?
- For "acts of service": Do you notice others' needs and pitch in to help by washing their car, folding laundry, going to the store, or whatever their needs might be? Are you delighted to help, not grumbling for having to do it?
- For "physical touch": Do you show appreciation and affection through hugs, embraces, touching the person's arm, or patting him on the back?

- For "giving gifts": Do you spend time thinking about just the right thing to buy or make for people, anticipating the sheer joy of seeing them enjoy the anticipation and reality of your gift?

We can communicate in any or all of these ways, of course. Yet everyone usually has one of these means as a primary method of conveying his or her love to another.

The second aspect of communicating love is a bit more difficult: understanding the love language of those around you. Young children aren't quite as hard to figure out. They usually look bored and disinterested when they receive something that isn't in their love language (whether a gift, time, a hug, help, or words of encouragement). Grandparents who haven't identified the child's love language are often offended by the "ungrateful little kid."

> *Grandparents who haven't identified the child's love language are often offended by the "ungrateful little kid."*

Older children and adolescents may be just as bored when their language isn't identified, but most learn to hide their disappointment and act like they are thankful even if they aren't. So to improve communication with these age groups, you need to ask questions like: "Phillip, would you rather have a nice gift for your birthday or a party with your friends?" Or, "Would you rather have me sew up your favorite shirt, or do you want to go with me to the store and buy you a new one?" Your grandchild may look at you wondering what planet you came from, but as you explain what you are learning about love, it will make plenty of sense.

Many people misunderstand the concept of "quality time." A few short minutes of focused attention on a child doesn't offset being absent most of the time. And on the other hand, simply being in the same room with a child for long periods of time cannot ensure "quality." When Debbie and I watch a television show with our girls, it isn't usually what I would call "quality time." However, if we discuss the plot and the decisions the characters made, then our time can be meaningful. Or, even better, we can turn off the television and play a game together. Interaction through discussions, homework, games, and anything else that stimulates meaningful conversation is a quality experience among family members.

Don't be surprised if you find out that you have tried the wrong language with some of your family members for years! Problems may have arisen, not because the other people are hard-hearted or ungrateful, but because you have misunderstood each other. As you begin to understand their languages, you can tailor your actions and words to touch their hearts. You may have to make some changes, but that's what love does: It takes the initiative to reach out and make a difference.

THE POWER OF LISTENING

Listening to a grandchild can be a delight, but it can also be a challenge. The age of the child makes a big difference in how well he or she communicates. Small children usually delight in talking to parents and grandparents about even the smallest detail of their lives. They may chat away endlessly about a bug, a kid's show on television, or something that happened on the playground. Before long, it's easy for an adult to lose concentration. Listening to a small child requires tenacity of focus so we can pay attention, and perhaps, direct the conversation a bit.

On the other end of the spectrum, high school students are in the process of pulling away from their parents and other adults. (*Individuating* is the psychological term.) While in the sometimes awkward process of creating their own identities, they don't want to be told how to do it! Quite often, they are willing to talk, but only on their own schedules. Some of these young adults are like deaf-mutes during the day when their parents and grandparents are available, but they walk in at midnight when we're sound asleep and want to talk about their deepest feelings, hopes, and dreams for the future.

If your grandchild wakes you up to talk, consider it a privilege and don't tell him to wait until tomorrow. That moment may not come again. Seize it now, shake the cobwebs out of your head, and jump into the conversation by asking a few follow-up questions. Draw your grandchild out, and be thrilled that he chose you to talk to—even if it was an inconvenient time for you to have the conversation.

> *Draw your grandchild out, and be thrilled that he chose you to talk to—even if it was an inconvenient time for you to have the conversation.*

Listen with your heart as well as with your ears, especially with younger children. An event that seems like a crisis to them may be almost humorous to you, but don't laugh. Acknowledge the validity of the child's emotions and affirm your love. You may not be the first person the child has talked to, but he may need a different response than he has received so far. A youngster may pout and complain, "Jimmy got in line in front of me at the swing today." An older sibling might reply coldly, "Why don't you just grow up? That kind of thing happens every day. Next time, just push him out of the way." You also know it's not the end of the world, but you can empathize with the child's feelings and make him or her feel much better.

Sometimes an older child's hidden motive in such circumstances is to draw attention away from the younger sibling to his own problems: "Yeah? Well, you don't know what real problems are. I got a D in algebra today, just because I didn't understand the stupid teacher."

Again, if you're listening carefully, you can make a difference. Listening must be individualized, and your response must carefully consider the specific developmental stage and needs of each child. In many cases, sibling rivalry makes it difficult to address both children's problems at the same time. Take time for one, privately and attentively, and then address the needs of the other. That way, both get the attention they want and need, and you don't find yourself acting as a referee between two warring kids. If both of them have the same problem, you may elect to address both of them at the same time. But even then, their rivalry may dictate that you deal with each one in turn to avoid bickering, name-calling, and confusion.

Of course, listening means we use our ears much more than our mouths. In many cases when children need correction, they already know what they did wrong and what they need to do about it. They aren't looking for advice, and they certainly don't need a lecture or condemnation. They simply want to know that you care. That's all. If they want more than that, they'll ask for your help and perspective, and you can respond with kindness and respect.

"NONPOSSESSIVE WARMTH"

You may recall the previous use of the term "nonpossessive warmth," defined as genuine affection without controlling the other person. Young people, like all the rest of us, are hungry for this kind of relationship. In fact, most of us spend our lives looking for it, and we devote much of our time and energy compensating for the lack of it.

A few years ago, Cindy told me a story about how each year her small high school held a "Beauty Walk," a fund-raiser and beauty pageant for the girls in the school. She said that everybody knew which girls would be in the top three spots because those girls were undeniably the prettiest. Many of the other girls were hesitant to even enter the contest, but the sponsors applied pressure for all the girls to enter so their parents, grandparents, and other relatives would come—and write checks. So even though she didn't really want to participate, Cindy entered the Beauty Walk. She knew she wouldn't win. In fact, she was painfully aware that her weight and general appearance didn't meet most beauty contest standards.

That night, the first few girls who came down the aisle were the knockouts, and they received thunderous applause (along with catcalls from a few young men in the audience). As each girl was announced and stepped out to walk, the level of applause reflected her popularity and beauty. Finally, Cindy stood near the door with only one more person in front of her. That girl wasn't pretty, and the applause she received was polite at best. Cindy was sure the reaction would be about the same for her. She anticipated the shame and embarrassment that she would face in only a moment or two.

The seconds ticked by. She wanted to run and hide, but it was too late. Her name was called, and she stepped out into the glaring lights. The applause was again polite, but muted. As she approached the end of the runway, the crowd was as silent as a tomb. Then out of the darkness in the audience, she heard her grandfather's voice, "That's my granddaughter. Cindy, you're beautiful to me!"

"He put my need of the moment above his own need. I was more important to him than his own reputation. I'll never forget that."

Cindy told me, "I've never forgotten the kindness my grandfather expressed to me when he spoke out that night. He may have sensed my embarrassment, maybe not. But he was willing to risk his own embarrassment among his neighbors to let me know that he loved me. He put my need of the moment above his own need. I was more important to him than his own reputation. I'll never forget that."

I've talked to many grandparents who tell me they show love to their grandkids with statements like, "They know I'll be there for them if they ever really need me," or, "If they get sick or hurt, they know I'll take care of them," or, "They know I'll get them whatever they need . . . as long as it's a *real* need."

Meeting needs in a crisis is certainly a positive thing, but the previous statements can be interpreted to mean, "If there's an emergency, I'll be there. If it's not a genuine, pressing problem, there's no need for me to get involved." Or grandparents may limit their expressions of love to specific events, such as Christmas and birthdays. Limited love, however, is not what young people need.

My parents and my mother-in-law look for every opportunity to show love to my girls, and they try to make every interaction as special and creative as it can be. I think they spend time talking and thinking about how to make these times as meaningful as possible, and they do a great job of it! They don't want to be stuck in a routine that, by its very repetition, drains the meaning and vitality out of the activities. This creativity takes time and energy, but my parents are reaping a rich harvest from the seeds of creative love they have planted.

Unconditional acceptance means that we allow grandchildren to fail without condemning or rejecting them. We use every failure, every moral lapse, and every difficulty as opportunities to teach the most important lesson about love: True love comes from the character of the one showing love, not from the characteristics of the one who is loved. What a difference this makes in our relationships! Instead of turning up our noses, blaming and condemning, or gossiping behind their backs, we express genuine compassion toward young people in a strong, appropriate way. That's the kind of love and grace Jesus showed us. If we want our grandchildren to experience the grace of God, we need to demonstrate grace ourselves and become the channels of God's grace to them.

When do young people need grace? When they are making straight A's and are the king or queen of popularity? No, they need it most when they are least attractive or when they have failed miserably. Extending grace means that we don't bring up their failures or sins over and over again to pressure them to change. We don't vent our own embarrassment over what they've done. And we don't show favor or compare one grandchild to another in an attempt to manipulate them. I've heard grandparents say things to a grandchild like, "If you could only be more like your cousin. He is doing so well in school, and he's not doing drugs. Why can't you be more like him?" Those words may be intended to give direction and motivation, but comparison tears a person down instead of building him up, and it causes tension between the two who are compared. Comparison and competition create a destructive fear/hope response. The person is afraid of being condemned again, and he desperately hopes to look good and be compared favorably, so he is easily manipulated . . . for a while. Sooner or later, however, he will see through this charade, and he will walk away from it—

and from those who used it to control him.

Comparison communicates the message: If you perform well, you will be loved, but if you perform poorly, love will be withheld. Many people long for love so much that they spend the rest of their lives trying to win approval. Everything they say, everything they do, and every choice they make is measured by a single standard: How can I get the approval of those I value? A grandchild who is compared unfavorably learns to resent the grandparent, but just as destructively, the one who is compared favorably learns to put others down. Ultimately, both lose. And the grandparents also lose because one either fears or despises them, and the other takes them for granted.

Be careful not to let your personal interests dictate your attitudes toward your grandchildren. I know a basketball coach who has a grandson who is not athletic at all. Throughout the boy's early life, the grandfather took him to games and tried to teach him the sport, but the boy only wanted to play the piano and sing. Different interests aren't wrong at all, and a grandparent who suggests they are can devastate a young life. This talented young man grew up feeling inferior (and sissy) because he wasn't the person his grandfather wanted him to be.

Look for what your grandchild does well, and affirm it. If he enjoys the things you enjoy, that's a bonus.

Comparison communicates the message: If you perform well, you will be loved, but if you perform poorly, love will be withheld.

If not, learn to appreciate his interests. Study your grandchild's strengths and talents. Watch and listen so you can talk intelligently and encourage him in his pursuits. You will both be better off for it. We naturally gravitate to the grandchildren who have interests like our own, but don't let that stop you from reaching out and loving each one, especially those who are wired differently than you are.

I've talked to many grandparents who refrained from getting involved with one of their grandkids because "she never asked me." In many cases, one grandchild had made clear requests to go to ballgames or the zoo, to read a book, or to do any of thousands of other activities. In families, however, there is often an introvert for every extrovert, a shy, retiring child who doesn't demand attention and doesn't make many requests. Does this child need less time? No. Does she need less attention and affection? No, not at all, but she doesn't verbalize her needs as openly or as often as her extroverted siblings. Don't be fooled by thinking the absence of a request is a sign you aren't wanted. Know the unique personality of each child, and learn each one's communication patterns.

We need to show the most grace when our grandchildren are in the biggest trouble or the deepest pain, such as:

- when they are out of control;
- when they won't listen;
- when they quit trying;
- when they walk away;
- when they blame us for their problems; or

- when they can't or won't appreciate how much we are giving to them.

There's a catch, though. If we haven't shown love during the good times, grandchildren may not accept our love in the hard times. We need to understand ourselves and make adjustments. For example, some grandparents gravitate to the needy grandchildren and neglect the ones who are doing well. Other grandparents shower their attention on the exceptional student or gifted athlete, and avoid the problem kids in the family because of

> *If we haven't shown love during the good times, grandchildren may not accept our love in the hard times.*

feelings of embarrassment or inadequacy to help. In both extremes the grandparents need to make changes and demonstrate love to all of their grandchildren. Yes, their needs are different, but each one is a dear child in the family and deserves an equal measure of kindness and compassion.

A GRANDPARENT . . .

Most of us are familiar with Paul's beautiful words about God's love in 1 Christians 13. I want to paraphrase them here to show what unconditional love should look like in the hearts and lives of grandparents.

"A grandparent suffers long and is kind; a grandparent does not envy; a grandparent does not parade himself, is not puffed up; does not behave rudely, does not seek his own, is not provoked, thinks no evil; does not rejoice in iniquity, but rejoices in the truth; bears all things, believes all things, hopes all things, endures all things. A grandparent never fails" (paraphrase of I Cor 13:4-8).

Paul lists the qualities that comprise Christian love, and I urge all grandparents to adopt and apply these characteristics of genuine compassion. Unconditional love is never out of season; it never is out of place. It has the power to change lives.

Love that is only expressed during good times isn't the real thing at all. Jesus spoke about that when He said, "If you love those who love you, what credit is that to you? For even sinners love those who love them. . . . But love your enemies, do good, and lend, hoping for nothing in return; and your reward will be great, and you will be sons of the Highest. For He is kind to the unthankful and evil. Therefore be merciful, just as your Father also is merciful" (Luke 6:32,35-36).

We can apply Jesus' directive by loving our grand-children when they embarrass us, or when they are unthankful, or when they do evil things. If we love them at these times when they are least lovable, we demon-strate the incredible grace of God, and we will receive, Jesus promised, a reward. What kind of reward? I'm not sure. Perhaps it will be stars on our crowns in heaven, but a more immediate reward may be the joy of seeing a life changed, for today and for eternity. That seems like a much better reward than any star!

WHY WE FAIL TO LOVE

We may fail to love for many reasons. In most cases, we have every intention of expressing affection, but our intentions are blocked by our fears, our hurts, or the unexpected rejection of the one we are trying to love. Remember, genuine love comes from the character of the lover, not from the characteristics of the one loved. If we limit our love to those who are lovable, we will miss numerous opportunities to make a positive difference. But if we draw on God's unlimited resources of forgiveness, kindness, and grace, His love can spill out into expressions of grace to our grandchildren, no matter how they act.

We fail to love when we:

- give or withhold our attention in order to manipulate a person;
- refuse to get involved because it's too much trouble;
- hold back because we're afraid of being hurt by someone;
- demand that our love be returned in kind;
- fear our children or grandchildren will take advantage of our efforts;
- use comparison as a tool to build one person up and put another down;
- sidestep the conflict between the parents in a divorce or strained marriage; or
- set expectations the grandchild must meet to win our affection.

Each of these reasons reflects our own failure, not that of our grandchildren.

Each of these reasons reflects our own failure, not that of our grandchildren. Our own failure to drink deeply of God's love leaves us spiritually and emotionally empty, and we're left with only bitterness, comparison, and blame. Our fear of being hurt again keeps us locked in our shell. This withdrawal protects us to some degree, but it also prevents us from experiencing the joy of giving and receiving love.

LOVE IS NOT JUST A FEELING

One of the most common fallacies in our culture is that love is first and foremost a warm feeling. Romantic scenes on television and in the movies are full of passion and kindness. Certainly, love may be expressed with these kinds of feelings, but many times it won't. Love is primarily a choice to put someone else first, to put another's needs in front of our own, to sacrifice our own convenience for the sake of another person's good.

How do we evaluate the depth of Jesus' love for us? Not by hearing the warmth of His words or seeing the sparkle of His smile. We comprehend the wealth of His love (to the extent that we are able) by realizing how much He gave when He didn't have to. In Gethsemane before He was arrested, He anticipated the pain and suffering of the cross, and He wanted to avoid it. He prayed, "O My Father, if it is possible, let this cup pass from Me" (Matt 26:39). Have you ever felt like that?

None of us has experienced the weight of responsibility in the same way Jesus did, and none of us has been called to sacrifice as much for the sake of others. But Jesus opened His heart and was tenaciously committed to do whatever it took to show love to you and me. So He continued His prayer, "Nevertheless, not as I will, but as You will." A few hours later, He went to the cross to suffer and die for all humankind. It was the character of the Lover that demonstrated the depth of love in the heart of God, not the characteristics of the loved.

We didn't deserve God's love. That's what grace is all about. Perhaps your grandchildren don't deserve your love, either. Each of us has done things that displeased God, but Jesus didn't give up on us. He chose to love us anyway. If we experience even the faintest glimmer of His monumental, wonderful love for us, we won't quit either. We will choose to love our grandchildren.

In this chapter we have looked at the heart of love. In the next chapter we will examine some specific messages to help us communicate that love.

REFLECTION

1. Have you written a letter to your grandchildren expressing your unconditional love? If not, what would you want to say to each one?

2. What is your love language? (Quality time? Words of affirmation? Acts of service? Physical touch? Giving gifts?)

    What is the love language of each of your grandchildren, and what are some specific things you can do to communicate your love for them in their own languages?

3. Who are the people in your life who are easy to listen to?

Who are the ones who are hard to listen to? Explain.

What can you do to be a more patient and persistent listener?

4. Write your own definition of "unconditional accept-
    ance." How is it expressed in practical ways? What
    is its origin? How does it affect both the one being
    loved and the one showing love?

5. How have you seen the effects of comparison:
    . . . In your own life?

    . . . In the lives of your immediate family members?

    . . . In the lives of your grandchildren?

6. How do our own fears, hurts, and needs keep us from loving?

7. What will it take for you to experience God's love more fully so you can express it more effectively to others, and specifically, to your grandchildren?

CHAPTER 5

The Communication Principle: Ways of Saying "I Love You"

❦

"Love is an act of endless forgiveness, a tender look which becomes a habit."—Peter Ustinov

God has created every person with a desire for love and significance. If we cut through all the surface layers of what we say and what we do, we will see these two desperate needs at the core of every person.

TRYING TO FILL THE HOLE

We either operate from a position of strength and security, with confidence that we are loved and significant, or we make desperate choices attempting to fulfill these two fundamental human needs. In the words of Mickey Gilley's song, too often we find ourselves "lookin' for love in all the wrong places." The attempt to fill the hole in their lives drives some people to please others, some to prove themselves, and others to hide.

The drive to please others

Some of us—whether grandparents, parents, or children—live for a kind word or any sign of affirmation.

127

We tailor what we say and change what we do hoping to win the smile of someone else. That smile satisfies us for a moment, but we soon long for more. A frown or a critical word cuts like a knife, and we do everything possible to avoid that hurt again. Others' opinions become the focal point of our lives, and we become, in effect, puppets. Other people can make us dance when they pull our strings with their approval or rejection.

The drive to prove ourselves

Others try to fill the holes in their hearts by proving to themselves and others that they are valuable. These people have to win at whatever "game" they play. In business, they have to be the top salesperson, the CEO, or at least climbing the success ladder higher and faster than their peers. In families and friendships, they have to be in control and make the decisions. No matter which game they choose, they play to win. Success may be measured by dollars, titles, possessions, or prestige. If they succeed, they take the credit and make sure everybody else knows about it, but if they fail, they are quick to point the finger of blame at someone or something else. Some of these people are shrewd in their game-playing, but others take foolish risks in the hope of hitting it big just one time and establishing a reputation as a winner.

> *If they succeed, they take the credit and make sure everybody else knows about it, but if they fail, they are quick to point the finger of blame at someone or something else.*

The drive to hide

Some people have tried to please, but frowns and condemnation became too painful to bear. They have tried to prove themselves, but failure and the risk of failing again overwhelmed them. So now, instead of taking action, they avoid risk whenever possible. Many such people become very nice in the attempt to avoid conflict; others become almost invisible as they evade any meaningful interaction.

The more stress a family experiences, the more likely it is that their core needs of love and significance are not being met. Consequently, each person tries to compensate by pleasing, proving, or hiding. Individuals within the family may have very different coping styles. For example, a family with an alcoholic father may contain a wife who is a pleaser and lives to win affection from her husband and her children, an over-achieving child who is determined to never allow anyone to hurt him again, and another child who responds to her pain and confusion by withdrawing into her room as soon as she comes home from school.

Whenever you see someone who is driven to please others, you can be sure the person has some deep, unmet needs for love. When someone is driven to control and win, you can assume she is looking for security while trying to avoid failure and hurt. And when you see someone who is unwilling to voice an opinion and hides (literally or emotionally), you can be sure that person feels broken and hopeless. These people need your active compassion.

TWO STATEMENTS

Two simple statements, if communicated with authenticity and creativity, meet the heart's deepest needs: "I love you" and "I'm proud of you." These two short statements can bring relief and rejoicing to a child who longs for someone, maybe a grandparent, to be thrilled with him and communicate that he is the delight of that person's life. Even talented and attractive children need to be loved for who they are, not for their looks and accomplishments. Unconditional love leads to confidence, but conditional acceptance creates a performance-based security that the child fears will disappear at his or her next failure.

Look for character qualities to affirm, not just skills and appearance. Be as specific as possible. Acknowledge qualities such as mercy, kindness, tenacity, optimism, integrity, and leadership. Don't just notice and name these traits, but nurture them as well.

Acknowledge qualities such as mercy, kindness, tenacity, optimism, integrity, and leadership. Don't just notice and name these traits, but nurture them as well.

For example, a grandmother saw that her 12-year-old grandson was struggling in school. His grades were falling and he was developing a strong and destructive sense of failure. His parents tried everything they could think of to change his direction. They used incentives like money for better grades and threats when the positive incentives didn't work. They forced him to stay in his room for two hours each day to study, and they paid for tutors to help him. Each thing they tried ultimately failed, and each failure was another nail in the coffin of this boy's sense of confidence. Soon he started to act in anger at home and at school. His grandmother was supportive and positive during all these attempts, but when she realized that the boy was losing confidence, she determined to take action herself.

She invited him to her house, where she didn't even mention his grades or homework or anger. Instead, she talked to him about baseball, his favorite sport. They talked for a long time about players, batting averages, and the hopes for his team that year. His eyes brightened, and he seemed to relax a bit. That was all they talked about that day, and she gave him a hug when it was time for him to go home.

Over the next few weeks, the two of them had many talks, and during that time, she gradually began to mention the wonderful character qualities she saw in him. Instead of complaining about his failing grades, she affirmed him for his memory of baseball statistics. Instead of reminding him of how often he'd failed in school, she expressed her sheer joy at being in his presence. And he soaked it in. His confidence gradually came back, and he started doing better in school. His parents and teachers marveled at the change, but they couldn't figure out what had happened to him. Even he didn't realize that his grandmother's careful affirmations were giving him renewed confidence and hope.

At no point in all of this did his grandmother tell him, "I'm working on a program to build your confidence and turn your life around." No, she very quietly took time to notice his abilities, name them for him, and nurture them in delightful conversations. He felt loved and significant as he saw how much his grandmother valued him. And she doesn't even like baseball!

It's easy to feel disgusted when we encounter arrogant young people. They seem to have the world by the tail and not need anybody or anything. Many of us notice depressed, withdrawn, out-of-control children and immediately realize they have problems, but the cocky kids need love, too. In fact, children who have to brag about themselves are screaming about their insecurity and fears. They use their cockiness as a shield to keep people away, to control others, and to prove their value.

I've noticed young people in many churches who seem arrogant until they are approached by adults who see through their self-assured act. On numerous occasions, I've seen a big, burly, cocky football player walk in with the attitude of, "I'm better than you, and you'd better stay away from me." But when a gentle, older lady gives him a hug, the facade of arrogance cracks and falls away.

We get pretty good at hiding our desperation with all manner of defense mechanisms, but we melt when genuine love is expressed to us.

Every person longs to be loved. We get pretty good at hiding our desperation with all manner of defense mechanisms, but we melt when genuine love is expressed to us. Those who please others to win approval need to know they don't have to dance on puppet's strings to be loved. Those who are driven to succeed need to know they are secure and lovable even if they fail. And those who avoid risks at all cost need to know that someone's love can help them relax, enjoy relationships, and experience adventure in life.

Children watch to see if adults notice them. Richard is a 12-year-old boy who attends our church. My friend Lane brings Richard to church each week because Richard's father is disabled and his mother has moved away. Richard, even more than most children, longs for attention. Last Christmas, our worship leader asked several adults and children, including Richard, to write a few sentences about what Christmas means to them. On the Sunday before Christmas, each person stood in front of the congregation and read what he or she had written. When it was Richard's turn, his message was rich and meaningful.

Before the service, Lane had told me that Richard greatly valued the opinion of any authority figure in his life. I wanted to encourage him, so after the service, I said, "Richard, I want to talk to you for a minute." I could tell from his initial apprehension that most of the adults who had told him that had followed up with correction and criticism. But we sat down and he gave me a chance to talk to him.

I looked into his eyes and said, "You probably know that I am a speaker and make my living in communications. Richard, I know what makes a good speaker, and I want to tell you: You have very good communication skills. You are articulate (I had to define the word for him, but he didn't seem to mind), and you express your thoughts very clearly. With skills like yours, you have unlimited potential to make a difference in many people's lives." Richard's smile beamed from ear to ear. A few minutes later he was repeating to everybody who would listen what I had said to him. And my few words of encouragement seemed to have a lasting effect. Some adults in his life have told me that since that day, Richard has more confidence in giving book reports in front of the class. She also affirmed his speaking skills, and has seen his grades improve and his confidence soar.

BE SINCERE

My words to Richard that Sunday morning were genuine and sincere. If he had bumbled his way through his message, I would have tried to find something else (anything!) on which to compliment him. I could have said simply, "Good job, Richard," but that wouldn't have had the impact of a carefully considered, focused affirmation that also included hope for his future. The young man had shown real promise in his brief reading. I noticed what he did well, named it so he could put a handle on his skill, and nurtured it by giving him hope that he could use that skill the rest of his life. And God used those few minutes to change a life. I'm not even related to Richard. If God can use me to affect this boy's life in such a profound way, how much more can He use the wise words of a grandparent who has a stronger connection and more love for a child?

The messages grandparents communicate to their grandchildren play a formative role in shaping the present and the future for those young people. The confidence children acquire from such encounters gives them a solid foundation for making sound, wise decisions instead of pleasing, proving, or hiding. And the security grandparents impart to children continues into the next stages of the child's life: the quality of his marriage, relationships with her own children, and so forth. If nobody else is providing such vital encouragement for young people, a wise and warmhearted grandparent can.

> *If nobody else is providing such vital encouragement for young people, a wise and warmhearted grandparent can.*

We have a somewhat warped view of the role of grandparents today. In many ways, that role has seriously eroded during the past 50 to 75 years, and in the last decade or two, grandparents have been all but forgotten. In past generations, grandparents played a very significant role in shaping young lives. That can still be true today, but their efforts now work against the grain of the culture.

Even children with strong, stable parents benefit from the wisdom and warmth that grandparents can provide. The stresses on children today are enormous: competition for colleges, efforts to look like the models on television, pressure to become sexually active, and countless other factors. In addition, divorce and frequent moves have taken away some of the most powerful supports the traditional family has known. All of these stress factors mean that the positive influences of grandparents have never been more needed than they are today. In fact, a grandparent's influence can be the ultimate difference between success and failure for the child.

MODELING HOPE

As we have seen, attitudes are "more caught than taught." Even more important than encouraging words is a positive model for young people to see. Those who analyze communications say that the actual words constitute only seven percent of the message the other person receives. The other ninety-three percent of what is communicated comes from body language, tone of voice, and gestures. Our words are important, but our words alone are not enough. Messages from the heart will include both verbal and nonverbal means to communicate more powerfully.

One of the most important gifts we can model for our grandchildren is an attitude of thankfulness and hope instead of self-pity and whining about all the things that are wrong in life. Some people, and particularly older people who have seen plenty of hard times through the years, make self-pity a competitive sport. They hear a friend's story of heartbreak and calamity, and they have to tell one that is just a little worse. Friends compete with one another to dig up the most sordid tale of woe, and in the process, they develop the habit of focusing on the negative. Do you know any people like this? Of course you do. We all know them. I just hope we don't see one of them when we look in the mirror!

Some grandparents express regret and self-pity when they compare themselves with others who have made more money or have had different opportunities. I've heard people lament, "If I hadn't been raised on the farm, I could have had a better education and made more of my life." Or, "If Daddy didn't have to work so hard, I'd have been able to spend more time with him." Or, "If I'd married somebody as good as my sister did, I'd be sitting pretty like she is today." These and countless other statements attempt to justify someone's current difficult situation by blaming the past. But blaming circumstances or other people creates a victim mentality and fosters self-pity in those who are exposed to such a poisonous attitude.

However, most of us also know people who are tenaciously grateful. They are "I see the glass half full" people who find something to be thankful for, no matter what is going on. I'm not talking about someone who is foolishly optimistic and is sure "everything will always be fine." That's simply not true. I'm talking about those who have a deep, abiding hope in the goodness and greatness of God and who trust in His kindness and sovereignty. Such people know that God often weaves His master plan using both blessing and calamity. They aren't shocked when troubles come because they trust that God will use even problems to shape lives and give wisdom.

In his book, *Reaching for the Invisible God*, Philip Yancey recounts that St. Basil's faith was described as "ambidextrous" because he welcomed pleasures with the right hand and afflictions with the left. He was convinced that God's design for him included both blessings and challenges.[7]

As examples for our grandchildren, this perspective is both refreshing and powerful. It is not just blind, superficial optimism. Kids see through that, and they

---

7 Philip Yancey, *Reaching for the Invisible God*, (Zondervan, Grand Rapids, Michigan, 2000), p. 69.

are repulsed by it. Rather, this is a wisdom that is forged on the anvil of suffering by the hammer of insight. Learning from our afflictions as well as our good times can be a painful process, but it produces wisdom and hope that is both sweet and strong.

All of us have experienced hard times. The question is: How did we allow those difficulties to shape us? Did we come away with a heart of hope and thankfulness, or did we become bitter and cynical? Whatever was produced in our hearts is what comes out of our mouths and is represented in our actions. And that's the model we provide for our grandchildren.

Instead of lamenting the hardships we have experienced, we can search for the good in them. We might conclude, "I had to work from dawn to dusk on my father's farm, and it was really hard. But the experience taught me some valuable lessons that have shaped my life. I learned to work hard even when nobody's watching, and I've seen the fruit of my labor in full bins of corn during harvest. I've also learned to appreciate the value of nice things. Since I worked so hard to get them, I may even appreciate them more than someone whose life was a bit easier." Such a perspective acknowledges the reality of hardship, but it has a very positive interpretation of the events.

Even if we have perceived ourselves as victims for many years, it's not too late to change. We can identify those destructive currents in our lives, uncover the pains of the past, and grieve the losses. And with time, we acquire wisdom—and an attitude of gratitude. We will stop blaming circumstances, parents, spouses, the government, and other people for not meeting our needs. A new thankfulness will replace the bitterness, and we will become a fresh source of hope for our grandchildren.

Grandkids watch to see how their grandparents handle crises: financial difficulties, health problems, or the death of a close family member. They're looking for an authentic response to the harsh reality as well as a never-dying glimmer of hope and faith that God has a good and gracious purpose in every event in our lives. Grandchildren take note if they see this combination of authenticity and hope, and they learn to respond in the same way when they face struggles in their own lives.

Make no mistake. Your grandchildren are watching you to see how you respond. You may think they don't care. You may think they don't even notice at all, but they do. You are an example for good or ill. The attitude you exhibit today is likely to show up in a grandchild's life tomorrow. Be aware of the powerful influence you have, and make the necessary changes to create a legacy of hope.

> *Make no mistake. Your grandchildren are watching you to see how you respond.*

CREATIVE CONNECTIONS, NOT PERFECTIONISM

A few years ago, a friend asked me to speak in Cedar Bluff, Alabama. The town is small and without a hotel. A widow, Mrs. Gunn, invited our family to stay with her. At the time, it was just Debbie, me, and our still-young daughter Maegan. Mrs. Gunn had a grown daughter, but no grandchildren.

The first night, Mrs. Gunn announced, "Tomorrow Maegan and I are going to bake some cookies." That next afternoon, it was time to bake. Debbie volunteered to help, but Mrs. Gunn smiled and said, "Thank you, but this is a job for Maegan and me." Little Maegan looked at her mom, Debbie nodded, and the two bakers went into the kitchen together. Debbie and I took that opportunity to run some errands. When we returned, the kitchen was a maze of messy bowls and used cookie sheets. Batter was splattered on every counter and a few places on the floor. It was a mess! But Maegan and Mrs. Gunn were having a great time. In a few minutes, they presented us with a wonderful plate of warm cookies. Some of the cookies were the size of quarters, and some were as big as saucers. That made no difference at all to Maegan and Mrs. Gunn, or to Debbie and me. The goal of the afternoon had been accomplished: The loving lady and the little girl had a ball together baking cookies!

That was a wonderful and memorable experience for Maegan. For weeks, she vividly recalled that afternoon, and she enjoyed telling every detail of their exploits in cookie-making. Mrs. Gunn's patience and joy with her gave Maegan confidence that day. Some ladies would have been protective of their kitchens. They would have carefully controlled every step to keep things clean, included the exact amounts of each ingredient so the cookies tasted just right, and made the little girl watch most of the time instead of pitching in up to her elbows in dough. If Mrs. Gunn had been that uptight, Maegan probably would never have recalled that day again, and it would have had no impact (no positive impact, anyway) on her young life. Yet her experience was so positive that if she had broken the blender, cracked the bowls, burned up the stove, and started a fire in the kitchen, I gladly would have paid the damages.

A grandparent's perfectionism communicates the undesirable message: "You'll never measure up." The compulsive need to control kills the joy of the experience and the warmth that it could produce between the two people, and time spent together becomes a negative recollection in that child's life. The freedom Maegan experienced with Mrs. Gunn gave her joy, built a lasting love, and actually made her aware of doing things the right way. It could not have been a more positive experience for a young girl.

> *A grandparent's perfectionism communicates the undesirable message: "You'll never measure up."*

BE OBSERVANT

Some grandparents live thousands of miles from their grandchildren yet know them intimately, and some live in the next room but don't have a clue what's going on in their grandkids' lives. Authors Gary Smalley and John Trent remind us: "Physical proximity does not equal personal knowledge."[8] When telemarketing companies want information about prospective clients, they often use survey techniques. Grandparents have a far

---

8 Gary Smalley and John Trent, *The Blessing*, (Thomas Nelson Publishers, Nashville, Tennessee, 1986), p. 103.

more valuable way to determine what's going on: eyes to see and ears to listen.

Notice what brings joy or sorrow to your grandchild. Pay attention to the things that she does in her spare time, the kinds of people and activities she enjoys, and the things that cause stress and fear. Ask probing (but non-threatening) questions, pleasant ones at first, and eventually ones that may expose more painful feelings. Use open-ended questions that don't have a specific, short answer, and seek the child's opinion, such as, "Why do you think Sarah responded that way in class?" When she responds, don't correct her, and don't even offer your opinion unless you are asked. As the relationship moves to a deeper level and trust is established, there will be plenty of opportunities to share your thoughts.

Smalley and Trent offer six questions to guide parents and grandparents in being more observant about young lives in their care:

1. What do the youngsters most often daydream about?
2. When they think ahead to their years as a young adult (age 20 to 30), what would they really enjoy doing?
3. Of all the people they have studied in the Bible, who is the person they would most like to be, and why?
4. What do they believe God wants them to do for humankind?
5. What type of boyfriend or girlfriend are they most attracted to, and why?

6. What is the best part of their school day, and what is the worst?[9]

Become a student of your grandchild. Go slowly. Notice the joys and griefs, the successes and failures, and what makes that dearly loved child tick. As you move to deeper levels of understanding, both of you will benefit from the joy of loving and being loved.

AVOID COMPETITION WITH PARENTS

One of the most common problems in extended family relationships arises when grandparents and parents compete for the children's love. Let's face it, all of us are needy people, and we all want to feel the warmth of someone's love. Too often, grandparents try to fill up the hole in their own lives by winning love from the grandkids at the expense of the parents. They sometimes compete for affection by giving presents that are more expensive than the parents can afford.

In one family I know, the parents have asked their son on several occasions what he wanted for Christmas or his birthday. After learning what he wanted, they went shopping to buy it. However, the grandparents also asked their grandson what he wanted. They not only bought him a more expensive, more top-of-the-line gift, but they also gave it to him as a "surprise" the day before Christmas or his birthday. The justifiably upset parents confronted the grandparents, who tried to excuse themselves: "Well, we just wanted to be the ones who gave that present to him this year. You can get him something else."

---

9 Smalley and Trent, *The Blessing,* p. 109.

When the parents continued to express their displeasure, the grandparents angrily exclaimed, "You're not going to tell us what we can get our own grandson!"

Competing for a child's affections says much more about us than about the child or the ones we are competing against. It shouts that we are desperately needy people who want to be loved. But if competition is our standard procedure of getting that love, we foster hurt and distrust instead of love.

Competing for a child's affections says much more about us than about the child or the ones we are competing against.

Grandparents can also compete for time and attention by planning an activity with the children that conflicts with the parents' plans. For instance, I know an older man who has the finest bass boat in the county, and his grandson loves to go fishing with him. Almost every Saturday in the spring and summer, the grandfather invites the boy to go fishing. The boy's father works hard and is off only on Saturday. He wants to do something with his son, but he doesn't enjoy fishing. When he suggests that he and his son do something else together, it puts the boy in the awkward position of having to choose between two men competing for his attention.

Of course, the conflict could be easily resolved if the father and grandfather talked honestly and were willing to compromise, but they aren't willing. The grandfather jealously guards his time with the boy and uses the boy's desire to be with him as a badge of honor . . . and as a club to hurt his son. Quite often, the issue is not just *what* happens, but the underlying motive of *why* people make the choices they do. A father should never have to compete with his own dad for his son's attention.

Another common point of conflict and competition between parents and grandparents is over the rules governing the child. Bedtime, curfew, homework, the amount and content of television, use of toys, the strictness of discipline, and choices of food top the most-debated list, but the items shift and change depending on the age of the child. It is almost a universal truth that grandparents will defend their own son or daughter while accusing the son-in-law or daughter-in-law of being too strict or too carefree with the grandkids. After all, the son's or daughter's competency reflects the grandparents' parenting skills. Grandparents need to be careful not to take sides in disputes between parents on how to raise their kids.

Marriage counselors report that the four most common issues they deal with are finances, children, sex, and in-laws. Grandparents often meddle in at least three of these! When taking sides with one of the parents—usually your own child—you may feel that you're offering protection and support, but it creates another layer of confusion and distrust in the person's marriage. You can be a listening ear and offer some carefully worded wisdom, but even this can be misconstrued. In many cases, it's best to say, "I'm sorry, but I don't think it's

In many cases, it's best to say, "I'm sorry, but I don't think it's wise for me to get involved in a disagreement between the two of you."

wise for me to get involved in a disagreement between the two of you. I love and support both of you, and I'll pray that you find wisdom. It might be good for you to talk to a pastor or counselor to work this out."

Many parents try to enforce clear rules for the child's behavior with consequences for disobedience, but I've known grandparents who encouraged disobedience and told the child, "Make sure you don't tell your parents. We'll keep this our secret." I also know grandparents who, when they disagree with their son or daughter about a rule for the grandchild, exclaim to the child, "Your mother doesn't know what she's talking about!" Or they shake their heads, "Your dad. . . . He never has understood much about raising children." I've heard some grandparents, in a moment of anger or frustration, tell the grandchild some of the stupid and embarrassing things the parent did when he was a child.

One grandmother even told her granddaughter, "Well, you know your mother got pregnant and had to quit school. She had to marry your father, and now you see what's become of her. You don't want to end up like that, do you?" The grandmother claimed to be encouraging the girl to do right, but her real motive was to give the girl a reason to question the wisdom of her parents, and in turn, raise the credibility of the grandmother as the benevolent and wise authority figure. Such behaviors undermine the parents' authority and lead to devastating consequences down the road.

I can hear some of the grandparents reading these pages rising up in indignation: "But what if the parents are wrong? What if they *are* too strict?" Good questions.

The answer is not to make your own rules. The better solution is to talk honestly and calmly with the parents and come to an agreement. In the eyes of God and the government, the parents are responsible for the well-being of the child, so it is inappropriate for grandparents to defy their expressed wishes. When a grandchild comes to whine and cry about parents being unfair, don't give in. Comfort the child, but support the parents and affirm their authority.

If you disagree with the parents, go to them privately. Don't argue in front of the kids, don't roll your eyes, and don't criticize the parents. Make a hard and fast commitment to be supportive and to avoid changing the rules without the parents' permission, and stick to that commitment even if you don't feel comfortable with it. Most parents are willing to bend a bit if they realize you aren't trying to undermine them.

Of course, in rare and extreme cases, a parent's rules are abusive and clearly wrong. If faced with such a situation, take action to protect your grandchild. But in the vast majority of cases, the conflict is not over right and wrong, but over preference and opinion. One of the most important lessons a grandparent can impart to a child is to respect his parents. Then, when that child is an adolescent and has strong inclinations to "buck the system," he can remember the lessons his grandparents taught and respect his parents' wishes and values.

It is possible for the grandparents to have rules that are more strict than, or at least different than, those of the parents. The principle here is the same as before: Take time to talk honestly and calmly with the parents to be sure everyone understands and supports the rules, and explain those rules to the children.

For example, my mother didn't grow up around lakes or swimming pools, and I didn't learn to swim when I was a boy. Today, my girls swim so much and so well I think they are going to grow gills! When they are with my parents in the summer, they often want to go swimming, but my parents always say no. It is my task to explain to the girls that "no swimming" is the rule in my parents' house. They may not like it, but that's the way it is. I don't roll my eyes. I don't tell my girls that their grandparents are strange or anything like that, and I don't give them permission to sneak off to the swimming pool when my parents aren't looking. I support my parents' wishes and authority. I trust that my two little fish will someday benefit more from learning respect for authority than for having the immediate gratification of their desire to go swimming.

It gets even more complicated when two sets of grandchildren come to visit the grandparents, blending at least three separate and distinct sets of rules and expectations. Make sure you talk to both sets of parents to clarify expectations about bedtime or curfew, food, or anything else that is important, and communicate clearly so everybody is on the same page. Understanding

> *Make sure you talk to both sets of parents to clarify expectations about bedtime or curfew, food, or anything else that is important, and communicate clearly so everybody is on the same page.*

and clear communication will save a lot of heartache and prevent accusations later.

CELEBRATIONS

Now for the fun part. One of the most pleasant aspects of being a grandparent is to go to your grandchildren's ball games, birthday parties, and Christmas gatherings to celebrate with them. To make these even more special, think about each child's specific love language and tailor your celebration around that. The joy you experience in being each child's cheerleader will find expression in your voice, in your actions, and in your gifts. But also be spontaneous in your affections.

One of the commercials I like these days is for a heart medication. It shows a grandfather fishing on a riverbank. His grandsons run up and jump in the water in front of him. The boys, splashing and having a ball, yell to the older man, "Come on, Grandpa! Jump in!" The older man puts down his fishing rod and takes a flying leap into the water with the laughing boys. Most of us would think, "No, I just put on these clean clothes, and I don't want to get them wet. And besides, what would your mother say if she knew I jumped in the river!" And a few of us would grouse, "Those boys ruined my fishing hole!" But in the commercial, the granddad didn't hold back. He jumped in, and they all had a wonderful memory.

The ideas for little extravagances are almost endless. A grandmother can take her granddaughter to have her nails done for the first time. A granddad can take his son to Bass Pro Shop and give him a twenty-dollar bill to spend there. Have your picture taken together. Go to a ballgame. Go to breakfast together. Send a flower. Write a letter. Give a rare coin. Compose a poem. Make a CD of the two of you singing. The older we get, the more we tend to adhere to a rigid routine. Break out of any ruts you have dug for yourself. Be creative to find expressions for your love through both carefully planned activities and spontaneous acts of affection.

COMPLEX COMMUNICATIONS

Family relationships have become much more complex because there are now many blended families, and some are blended two or three times over. Love transcends DNA. It is our great privilege and responsibility to shower affection and attention on young lives, whether or not our blood runs in their veins. If God has placed those people in our lives, we need to look at them through His eyes. Don't withhold the priceless gifts of love and affirmation. Give them liberally. Look for opportunities to encourage all the children and fill the holes, sometimes very deep, left by divorce, disease, and death. In some families, a single mother raises children with no help, or minimal help, from the absent father. In such cases, the grandfather is the only male figure in the children's lives, and he has to figure out what role he is to play: father or grandfather.

In many blended families, people normally relate to each other with jealousy and competition.

In many blended families, people normally relate to each other with jealousy and competition. Each broken and needy person jockeys for position and tries to compensate for the hurt and emptiness he feels. "Pleasers" are more likely to lose their identities in desperate attempts to win approval. Those who are driven to succeed are even more committed to dominate others and win at all costs. And those who normally hide from trouble to avoid more pain seem to evaporate entirely into nothingness.

Grandparents are often deeply hurt by the same traumas that broke apart their kids' lives, but instead of wallowing in the mire of jealousy and competition with the rest of the family, they can rise above it to demonstrate love and truth instead of hurt and manipulation. They can use the painful, stressful situation as a powerful tool to teach the most valuable lessons of life about grace, honesty, and integrity. This perspective requires insight and courage. Insight gives us the wisdom to see the situation with clarity, and courage gives us the energy and passion to make a difference in others' lives.

Sometimes love feels warm and wonderful, but sometimes love requires that we speak truth to those who don't want to hear it, show affection for those who don't deserve it, and stay calm when those around us are out of control.

In the next chapter, we will examine our need for courage and where we can turn for strength.

REFLECTION

1. How did your own grandparents communicate the two significant messages: "I love you" and "I'm proud of you"?

2. Take a look at each person in your family. Do you notice any (or all) of them trying to compensate for holes in their lives by pleasing, proving, or hiding? If so, give specific examples.

3. Think of each of your grandchildren. What character qualities can you affirm in each of them?

Which qualities are harder to identify than the others? Why do you think it may be even more important to identify and affirm these intangible qualities?

4. What are some specific ways you can nurture those qualities in each child?

5. Have you detected any competition concerning your grandchildren in your relationship with your son or daughter? Explain.

Have you experienced any competition with your son-in-law or daughter-in-law? Explain.

Do you ever feel you are in competition with the other grandparents? Explain.

6. How are rules defined and negotiated in your relationships with sons/daughters, sons-in-law/daughters-in-law, and other grandparents?

7. What are some ways you can celebrate your love for each of your grandchildren?

8. If you are in a blended family, what are the biggest problems you face?

How can "love transcend DNA" in your family?

How can you rise above your problems and be a light in the darkness to the people involved?

The Courage Principle: Providing Strength in Difficult Times

"Each man must have his 'I'; it is more necessary to him than bread."—Charles Horton Cooley

Franklin Roosevelt proclaimed that December 7, 1941, was "a date that will live in infamy." Almost everyone alive on that date can remember where they were when they heard about the Japanese attack on Pearl Harbor. Similarly, Boomers remember where they were when President Kennedy was assassinated.

Today's generation will remember where they were on September 11, 2001, when the suicide pilots crashed into the World Trade Center, the Pentagon, and the field in Pennsylvania. On that day, I vividly recall my wife coming in during our staff meeting to tell us that two planes had hit the twin towers. A few minutes later, the phone started ringing. Relatives wanted to know if I was on a plane, and other callers were trying to track down staff members who were scheduled to fly that fateful day.

Throughout the day, we watched the news to stay up on the developments. That afternoon schools dismissed their students, and children all across the country ran home to the arms of their parents. A few days later, I talked to some elementary school teachers, and they told me that most of the children in their classes instinctively called their grandparents as soon as they got home. I realized that's exactly what my own daughters had done. Melodi and Maegan needed the insight of someone they love and trust. As the world appeared to be coming apart at the seams, they needed their grandparents to give them hope and courage. Their questions focused on two concerns, "Are the terrorists going to hit our school?" and, "Are we going to die, too?"

A week or so later, I was scheduled to fly to a conference. That was a traumatic time for my girls. They wondered what might happen to me on the plane that day, and they turned to their grandmothers who told them, "It's going to be OK. Don't worry."

Grandparents are in a unique position to give insight and courage to their grandchildren. Kids instinctively know that their grandparents may not be hip to the latest styles, but those older people have something that is far more valuable: wisdom. Their wisdom, gained from years of experience, gives children courage to keep going even in the darkest times in their lives. When circumstances shake a child's confidence or when people attack his identity, a grandparent can provide the firm ground on which that child can stand.

Kids instinctively know that their grandparents may not be hip to the latest styles, but those older people have something that is far more valuable: wisdom.

EXPECTING AN EASY, SUCCESSFUL LIFE

Today's young people are the first generation to grow up with 100 channels on cable television all day every day. Their minds—and their values—are saturated with movies, comedies, sports, and commercials. The implied promise is that every problem can be solved in 30 minutes, or if it's really bad, in two hours. Programs like *Fear Factor* and *Survivor* portray only one winner with a majority of losers (and often, bad losers who whine about the other contestants). And commercials, as we all know, are designed to create dissatisfaction. They imply that we simply can't be happy unless we buy the products and services offered. Ad agencies have fine-tuned their art to create a cult following that supports the brands they promote. Movie stars and models are always gorgeous, and yet their appearance is presented as the norm that everyone should be able to achieve.

When young people realize they fall short of the standard of perfection, many of them simply give up. If they can't be the most beautiful or in first place, they don't want to even try. They quit.

Years ago I was a referee for high school basketball games, and during those years, I made a lot of friends among the coaches in Alabama. Several of these coaches have recently told me they are having problems getting students to even play the game. Students tell them, "We probably aren't going to win state this year, so why should I play?" And those coaches have noticed that players on teams that aren't in playoff contention often quit trying when the team is statistically eliminated. They don't want to come to practice, and they don't care about playing the remaining games. Winning is everything to today's kids. Their grandfathers were happy to be on a team; their fathers wanted to win, yet tried hard no matter what; but today's students have to win to stay motivated.

Young people need grandparents who can give them the courage to persevere even when they can't be number one. Winning isn't everything. Character is. Grandparents can teach young people the inherent value of tenacity and teamwork, qualities that will serve them well no matter how good or bad life becomes for them. Everyone experiences hardships from time to time: disease, misunderstanding, losing a job, having to move, and other kinds of stress and loss. If we expect everything to go well all the time, we panic when these difficulties hit, and many of us simply quit trying.

This wisdom is the root of courage. It gives perspective so they aren't devastated when things don't go perfectly, and it gives genuine joy instead of complacency when they experience blessings.

The recent economic downturn was quite a shock for many young people, as well as adults who had forgotten what it is like to lose a job or have a cutback in income. Most grandparents, though, have suffered through the cycles of boom and bust, of plenty and recession, of good times and bad. They don't get too elated during the good times, and they don't get too depressed during the bad. They have accumulated wisdom from all the hard knocks of their experience. This wisdom is the root of courage. It gives perspective so they aren't devastated when things don't go perfectly, and it gives genuine joy instead of complacency when they experience blessings.

I'm thankful my parents told me about times when they had no money and could hardly pay their bills. Those were hard times, but somehow they scraped enough together to get those bills paid and make it through. Their stories gave me a more realistic perspective about the ups and downs of life, and it showed me the grit that people have to possess to survive.

A lack of tenacity may be at the root of the high divorce rate today. If things don't go the way couples want, many simply quit trying. Years ago, quitting wasn't a common option. Couples found a way to stay together. Even after they realized they weren't going to have a fairy-tale marriage, they remained committed to one another "until death do us part." I'm afraid that today's young people, who are convinced that life should be easy and fun for them, may be even more likely to divorce than their parents. That would be a tragedy.

Bill Simrell is a friend of mine who exemplifies tenacious commitment in marriage through thick and thin. Several years ago, his wife began to be forgetful. After some tests, the doctors informed them that she had a rapidly deteriorating form of Alzheimer's disease. Soon she became homebound, helpless, and unable to recognize her own husband. Bill no longer had coffee in the mornings with his friends. He no longer could leave his wife to go to church. He couldn't even go shopping without finding someone to stay with her. But he never complained. He had been committed to her when they enjoyed love and laughter together, and he was just as committed to her when she was no longer the woman he had once known.

About a year ago, Bill's wife died. Some time later, Bill came to our home with another widower, Pat Brock, for Thanksgiving dinner. My daughters asked him question after question about what it was like to care for his wife, and Bill patiently told how he had loved and cared for her. After he left, Melodi exclaimed, "He took care of his wife like that, day after day, for *years!* Why didn't he put her in a nursing home? Why would anybody do something like that?"

I answered, "When Bill stood before the altar at their wedding, he vowed he would love her 'for better or for worse, in sickness and in health.' That's the commitment he made to God and to his wife that day, and that's the love he demonstrated for years." Bill didn't go into the marriage with the unspoken expectation that he would bail out if things got bad. The perseverance he demonstrated was built on the solid foundation of tenacious realism: Sometimes life isn't fair, but he had a steadfast commitment to love his wife no matter what. He sought no escape clauses, no parachutes. My daughters saw Bill's gracious and rock-solid commitment to his wife, and they are better people because they learned from his example.

WHY DO THEY NEED COURAGE?

We have identified many of the stresses in the lives of young people (and their parents). Mobility, fractured families, the rapid pace of life, and unrealistic expectations weaken their sense of stability. Let's look at a few of their problems in more detail:

They are tempted to give in to peer pressure.

Children, and especially adolescents, feel enormous pressure to fit in. The threat of being excluded or ridiculed by their peer group is enough to cause many young people to waver in their values and commitments.

They are tempted to give up.

If things don't go perfectly, many won't settle for "doing their best." The combination of heightened stress and unrealistic expectations lead many young people to take the easier road of passivity.

They are tempted to lash out.

Road rage, school violence, ethnic hatred, and other evidences of explosive anger fill the nightly news. Countless other forms of hostility fill conversations and hearts as young people seek revenge on those who hurt them.

They are tempted to look for the easy way.

Tenacity quickly disappears when people expect life to be easy and fun but instead encounter difficulties. Rather than setting clear goals and plodding along the often difficult road to achieve those goals, some young people keep looking until they find an easier path. The plague of cheating in our schools is an evidence of this phenomenon.

The courage grandparents have developed through years of experience can counter each of these temptations. By their words and examples, grandparents can shape the expectations of their grandchildren and provide vital

When a young person is ready to give up and give in because of fear, the look of hope in the eyes of a grandparent may be the only thing that keeps him going.

personal encouragement to keep young lives on the right track. When a young person is ready to give up and give in because of fear, the look of hope in the eyes of a grandparent may be the only thing that keeps him going. The trauma of divorce, moving to another city, failure, or tragedy can destroy a life if no one is there to impart courage. A grandparent can provide the strong hope that every event can become a stepping-stone to new insight and personal growth. Those lessons may not be enjoyable, but they are essential in chiseling a person of character.

In his best-selling book, *The Greatest Generation,* Tom Brokaw relates the story of a man who was blinded in World War II. Tom Broderick was a 19-year-old college student in 1942, but he wasn't willing to stay in college with a war going on. He quit school and joined the Merchant Marines. The pay and the food were good, but Tom was bored working on a supply ship, so he volunteered for the Army Airborne. His basic training went so well that he was offered a promotion and duty as an instructor. Tom turned those down because he wanted to be where the action was—in combat. In the summer of 1944, he was dropped into the Battle of Arnhem just after the Normandy invasion. The paratroopers were outnumbered, but they fought bravely. On the fifth day of the battle, Broderick's life changed in an instant. He told Brokaw, "I remember being in a foxhole and . . . I was lining up my aim on a German. I got a little high in the foxhole and I got a clean shot through the head [his own]—through the left temple." Miraculously, Tom survived the wound, but he couldn't see. For several days, the doctors told him his sight would return when the bleeding stopped, but finally, one of them told him the hard truth. He was blind, with no hope of regaining his sight.

Broderick was shocked and angry. He cried, he barked his rage at the doctor, and he became disoriented. The Army enrolled him in a rehabilitation course so he could learn Braille, but he quickly got frustrated. He left to go home and work for his dad's trucking business. He took orders over the phone, but he made too many mistakes, so he had to quit. Broderick realized he had to learn Braille, and he enrolled in that course, as well as one on the burgeoning insurance business. Soon he became a successful insurance agent by using the Braille he had learned, and he married a wonderful girl who saw past his disability and into his huge heart. Instead of wallowing in self-pity and blaming others for his misfortune, Broderick used his experience to help others. With some friends who had also been blinded in the war, Tom formed the Blind Veterans Association. He provided help and resources for discouraged men who needed those things very badly.

Brokaw relates, "Tom Broderick in so many ways embodies the best qualities of his generation. He was so eager to get involved in the war he enlisted in two branches of service. He was gravely wounded, but once he got over the initial understandable anger, he set out to be the best husband, father, businessman, and citizen he could be—sight or no sight. He didn't grow bitter and dependent on others. He didn't blame the world for his condition."[10] Tom Broderick's courage was an example and a motivation to his kids, his grandkids, blinded soldiers, and countless others throughout the years.

OVERCOMING SELF-PITY

Unrealistic expectations inevitably lead to self-pity, bitterness because someone has done us wrong, and the belief that we are helpless victims. All of us experience difficulties, sometimes severe and tragic ones, but the factor that makes or breaks us is our perspective on the event. If we see it as a step to something better, we can muster courage and hope, but if we see ourselves as helpless victims, we will wallow in bitterness and self-pity. One of the most important lessons a grandparent can teach a grandchild is the danger of self-pity.

One of the most important lessons a grandparent can teach a grandchild is the danger of self-pity.

Admiral James Stockdale was the highest ranking prisoner of war in the Vietnam conflict. For years he languished in prison with his days alternating between boredom and torture. Days turned to weeks, weeks turned to months, and months turned to years. Through those interminably long, grueling, hope-killing days, Stockdale was not rescued or released. It would have

---

10 Tom Brokaw, *The Greatest Generation,* (Random House, New York, 1998), pp. 17-24.

been easy to give up, but he refused. He firmly held to two perspectives: Retain faith that you will prevail in the end regardless of the difficulties, and at the same time, confront the most brutal facts of your current reality, whatever they may be. In his book, *Good to Great,* author Jim Collins calls this dual perspective on hardship "The Stockdale Paradox."[11]

Most of us tend to see problems from one perspective and exclude the other. We either have blind faith that "everything will be just fine" and hope that someone, somewhere, somehow will magically solve our problem, or we become overwhelmed with the pain of the reality and lose hope that there will ever be a solution. Either perspective without the other is shortsighted and will ultimately lead to discouragement and self-pity.

Pastor John Piper, author of *Desiring God,* offers insight about the nature of self-pity. He wrote:

> "The nature and depth of human pride are illuminated by comparing boasting to self-pity. Both are manifestations of pride. Boasting is the response of pride to success. Self-pity is the response of pride to suffering. Boasting says, 'I deserve admiration because I have achieved so much.' Self-pity says, 'I deserve admiration because I have sacrificed so much.' Boasting is the voice of pride in the heart of the strong. Self-pity is the voice of pride in the heart of the weak. Boasting sounds self-sufficient. Self-pity sounds self-sacrificing. The reason self-pity

11 Jim Collins, *Good to Great,* (Harper Business, New York, 2001), p. 86.

does not look like pride is that it appears to be needy. But the need arises from a wounded ego, and the desire of the self-pitying is not really for others to see them as helpless, but as heroes. The need self-pity feels does not come from a sense of unworthiness, but from a sense of unrecognized worthiness. It is the response of unapplauded pride."[12]

Those who wallow in self-pity want attention, and they want somebody to fix their problem. They whine about their situation and wait passively for someone to make them feel better and make their problem go away. Occasionally someone jumps in to help, but even then, nothing that person does is good enough, so the wallowing and blaming continue.

A strong, compelling sense of purpose is one of the strongest antidotes to self-pity. Someone who has a sense of destiny and a perspective that life has meaning is able to endure even the most difficult situation and use it for something good. A person who lacks that driving sense of purpose, however, drifts along at the mercy of life's inevitable winds and waves. If the winds blow gently, he is happy, but if storms rock his boat, he feels helpless. Those who know where they are going are not likely to be thrown off course for long. They may be battered by the wind and waves, and they may be confused about what to do at times, but they will find a way to get where they have determined to go. Grandparents must

---

12 John Piper, *Desiring God,* (Multnomah Books, Sisters, Oregon, 1986), p 250.

possess such a sense of purpose before they can impart it to a grandchild. They can't give away something they don't possess.

WHEN HELPING IS HURTING

When a grandchild is out of control or depressed, a grandparent has a double dose of emotional pain watching the child and his parents suffer through the problem. As we watch, we want to relieve the child's pain, the parent's pain, and our own hurt and helplessness. Great wisdom and courage are required to know and do the right thing.

As I have said so often in this book, a grandparent can offer comfort for a child like no one else in the world, but a point can be reached when helping actually hurts the child. To "encourage" means to give courage that leads to responsibility. If we protect a child from the consequences of his own behavior, or if we do things for a child that he needs to learn to do himself, we create "learned helplessness" in him. He

> *When a grandchild is out of control or depressed, a grandparent has a double dose of emotional pain watching the child and his parents suffer through the problem.*

learns that he can be passive and still get what he wants. This robs him of energy and drive, and it prevents him from learning from trial and error, perhaps the best teacher. Many well-meaning grandparents don't know where to draw the line. Some grandparents smother needy grandchildren in attention, protection, and help to make up for their own failures as parents, or perhaps, to compensate for their children's failures as parents.

Perhaps the clearest way to tell if we are too involved is to ask ourselves (and the grandchild) if we are making decisions for her that she needs to make for herself, or if we're doing things that she needs to do. As the child matures, she needs to shoulder more and more of the privilege and responsibility of making her own decisions. As long as we keep directing her choices, we are communicating the message, "You are incompetent. You can't be trusted to make decisions for yourself." Some of us are so afraid that she will make mistakes that we never give her the chance. This may eliminate a short-term problem, but it creates a huge long-term debacle because the message, "You are incompetent," becomes self-fulfilling. The child carries those feelings of incompetence into adulthood.

Of course, the age and development of the child and the nature of the problem determine how much help is appropriate. Younger children require more protection and nurture, but as they grow up, they need to become responsible young adults.

In his letter to the Galatian Christians, Paul gives us a very helpful distinction. He instructs them and us, "Bear one another's burdens, and so fulfill the law of Christ" (Gal 6:2). And almost immediately, he adds, "But let each one examine his own work, and then he will have rejoicing in himself alone, and not in another. For each one shall bear his own load" (vs 4-5). The "burden" in the first passage refers to those things that we can't handle on our own. We are instructed to care for those whose hurts and struggles are so heavy that they desperately need help. When we help such needy people, we are fulfilling the law of Christ to "love your neighbor as yourself."

The second passage, however, identifies a different type of burden: a "load." This is not an oppressive burden like a wagonload of bricks. It is more like a backpack. Each person is responsible to carry his own backpack—to make his own decisions and experience the joys and pains they will bring. When we carry someone else's backpack, we not only deprive him or her of what might be learned by the daily exercise of responsibility, but we also needlessly make life weightier for ourselves.

The rule of thumb is: What level of responsibility would you expect a normal, healthy person of that age to shoulder?

The lesson for grandparents in these passages of Scripture is to wisely differentiate between burdens where a grandchild requires your assistance and those that are simply a part of growing up. The rule of thumb is: What level of responsibility would you expect a normal, healthy person of that age to shoulder? Here are some examples to consider:

- Should you step in to protect an eight-year-old whose parent is violent? Yes, that is a burden a child cannot bear on his own. If a child is in danger from abuse, drugs, or violence of any kind, you are morally and legally obligated to intervene, whether it is your own grandchild or a kid down the street.

- Should you give money to a teenager? Maybe, maybe not. If the money is to provide necessities that the parents can't or won't provide, you probably should. But if the teenager simply wants the latest tennis shoes, he can get a job to earn the money. If he whines when you say no, then it is very likely you made the right decision.

- Should you have your 12-year-old granddaughter live with you while her parents go through a messy divorce? Probably not. She needs to be with her parents, even during this difficult time, but she also needs a large dose of her grandparent's wisdom and encouragement so she can think clearly amid the turmoil in her life.

- Should you give more lavishly to a hurting child than to one who is doing well? You may give the hurting child more time and attention, but not more presents or money. That child needs more love and encouragement, but tangible expressions can be misunderstood. The child may feel his or her pain is somehow being rewarded by the gifts. In addition, other grandchildren can get jealous, and your relationship with them can be harmed.

Some grandparents give time and money to grandkids to meet their own needs, not to meet the needs of the child. When we give to meet our own needs, we don't know when and where to stop, and we often give too much, hurting the child instead of helping him. Smothering is not loving. As the child grows, the most loving thing we can do is to speak the truth, be clear about the consequences, and clarify choices. We don't make decisions for adolescents, but we offer our wisdom and set them free to choose. Young people will make some mistakes. You did, I did, and they will, too. If we smother them with directives and make their decisions for them, they may become emotionally and volitionally impotent, incapable of making decisions for the rest of their lives. In their learned helplessness, they may beg and plead with a parent or grandparent to make decisions for them, but don't do it! Make clear distinctions between the overwhelming burden and the normal load, and don't carry your grandchild's backpack.

What can you expect when you stop smothering a young person with time, attention, and money? He won't like it! Passive people don't want to take responsibility. They make excuses, they whine, and they blame you for being mean or unloving. They will do whatever they can do to get you to fix them and let them be passive again. Expect that kind of response. It's coming.

In many cases where the parents and grandparents have vastly differing views of what is appropriate for a grandchild, a grandparent's role must be negotiated with the parents. No matter how much a grandparent wants to help, there is a limit to what he can do because the parents are still legally responsible for the child's welfare. If the disagreement becomes fierce, don't let the bonds be irreparably broken. Even if the parents

> *Leave the door open for a relationship with the grandchild by telling him that you love him and you are available whenever he wants your help.*

demand that you get out of their lives, leave the door open for a relationship with the grandchild by telling him that you love him and you are available whenever he wants your help. Maybe when your grandchild is older, he will contact you and step back into the relationship with you.

TRIANGLES

Some children know how to play their parents and grandparents like a drum. They have perfected the art of triangles, playing one against the other, making accusations and alliances to stir people up. If parents and grandparents are mad at each other, the child knows she can probably get whatever she wants from one side or the other.

A granddaughter may know her mother's mother doesn't particularly care for her son-in-law, the girl's dad. Perhaps she didn't want her beloved daughter to marry him, and she sees every problem in their marriage as his fault. The granddaughter can go to her grandmother and say, "I wonder why Dad is so mean to Mom." That sets the grandmother off, and her tirade against the man is long and loud! After a while, the girl suggests, "Grandma, don't you think Daddy ought to get me a car instead of spending his money on fishing? Don't you think he's being selfish?" Which side do you think the grandmother will take? She calls the daughter (not the son-in-law) and demands that she tell her "no-good bum of a husband" to give that dear girl a car. The whole family gets agitated and upset—except the girl. She knows exactly what she's doing!

Young people today know what buttons to push to get the attention of parents, grandparents, and other adults. They know the words "abuse," "sexual abuse," "incest," and other buzzwords get action. When a child goes to a grandparent and says, "Daddy is abusing me," the grandmother is in a catch-22. If she is suspicious but does nothing, and then finds the abuse is real, she has failed to protect her granddaughter. But if she reacts too quickly and accuses him when he has actually done nothing wrong, she looks like a fool and has eroded trust throughout the family.

Sometimes the best actions a grandparent can take are to watch and pray. Don't jump to conclusions. Instead, look for patterns of behavior in the alleged victim and the accused perpetrator. Talk to a pastor or counselor for additional insight, and get advice about how to handle the situation. You may find a very real, very deep problem that comes to the surface, or you may discover the accusation was a lie (or an extreme stretch of the truth) designed to manipulate the situation. But in either case, you will almost undoubtedly find someone, and maybe several people, with genuine hurts and anger that need to be addressed with grace and honesty.

Triangles can be broken, but it takes courage. I know a young woman who has a lot of trouble living within a budget. Her parents pleaded with her to be more frugal, and they gave her money time after time to keep her debt from ruining her credit rating. Finally, they realized all their money and all their lectures hadn't made any difference in their daughter's life. She was still just as irresponsible as ever, so they stopped giving her money.

It wasn't long before the young woman called her grandfather and pleaded for his help. She asked him not to tell her parents that she was asking him for money. He had plenty of savings, and he loved her dearly, so he wrote her a check for $1000. The very next day, she squandered the money at the mall. When the credit card bills came, she was maxed out again. She called her grandfather to ask him for more money, but he had learned his lesson. He first called her parents and found out that the girl's problem was long-term, and then he invited her to his house. He explained that he wasn't going to give her any more money because it would only prolong her lack of responsibility. She, of course, was furious and accused him of betraying her trust. He clarified that he hadn't said anything the first time she asked him, but when she asked again, he investigated and found out the truth. The triangle was broken because this grandfather cared more for the girl's long-term good character than for the instant gratification of receiving her thanks.

CLARIFY CHOICES AND CONSEQUENCES

One of the most significant services a grandparent can provide is the wisdom to clarify options and spell out the probable consequences of each one. People under stress don't think very clearly, and they often fail to realize they have several choices that could solve their problem. They just keep doing the same thing, hoping for different results. (That, by the way, is one of the definitions of insanity!)

Rational analysis, combined with bold action, can have marvelous results. Help a child understand the risks and benefits of each option by clearly articulating the consequences. And explain that consequences may be natural results of a choice, or they may be imposed by an authority figure, such as the police, a teacher, or a parent.

People under stress don't think very clearly, and they often fail to realize they have several choices that could solve their problem.

Christi is a teenager who had been doing drugs since her father left home five years ago. Her mother had tried to provide for Christi and her younger brother, but the combined stress of hurt, loneliness, working, and raising a family left her emotionally depleted. Christi tried to lose herself in drugs and find love in her relationships with boys. Her drug habit escalated from alcohol to marijuana to ecstasy to cocaine. She was arrested for possession twice. Her mother kicked her out of the house after the second arrest, so Christi went to her grandparents.

They welcomed her gladly and offered her a loving home. But the day after she arrived, they sat her down and told her, "Honey, we love you more than you will ever know. We've been praying for you your whole life, and especially these past five years since your Dad left. We know you're hurt and angry, and we know about the arrests. We are very happy to have you here with us, but you need to know a couple of things. You are a young adult, and we expect you to act like one. There will be no drugs brought into this house, or you'll have to leave. And if you get arrested, we won't bail you out. We expect you to do your part around here, and to treat us with respect, just like we will treat you."

Christi had grown accustomed to her mother yelling at her and her father being absent from her life. She certainly wasn't used to being treated like an adult. After a few minor incidents, like not washing her clothes for a week and leaving dishes on the counter a few times, things went very well. Then, one night, her grandfather got a call from the police. Christi had been arrested. The officer said, "Sir, you can come down and post bail."

The grandfather answered, "Thank you, officer, but no, I won't be coming."

The officer was surprised, "Her mother usually does, and uh, I thought you might want to."

"No. Thank you, officer. We have a deal, and Christi doesn't expect me to bail her out."

At her trial, Christi was found guilty, but was given probation. When she was released, her grandfather was there to pick her up. She was surprised to see him, but he told her, "Honey, I promised to treat you like an adult, not to abandon you. I love you enough to let you make your own choices, but you're still welcome at our home as long as you are willing to act like an adult. Are you coming home with me?"

She smiled and got in the car. She had some other rough moments over the next few months, but her grandparents understood their role and were able to make a difference in her life. They gave her clear choices and consequences, and God used them to turn a young woman's life around.

Another family had a 12-year-old son who came home from school every day and played on his computer. Even at supper, he didn't miss a beat. His mother would take him a plate and he would eat with his left hand while he had his right hand on the joystick. His grades gradually declined because he failed to do his homework. Each time his father would yell at him, the boy would run to his room, slam the door, and play on his computer. As time passed, the father would threaten to take away the computer, and the mother would cry and plead with the boy to shape up, but nothing changed and the father never followed through with his threats.

This scenario went on for months. Finally, the father asked his dad for advice. The grandfather already knew the situation, and he suggested that three options be offered to the boy:

1. He could set aside two hours each day to play on the computer, no more. And he had to get his homework done. If he played longer or if he failed to get his homework done, he forfeited his computer privileges for the next day.

2. He could play only one hour a day until he got his grades up and kept them up for a semester. At that point, he could play on his computer as much as he wanted as long as he maintained all A's and B's.

3. The parents could take the computer out of his room, and he could use it in a common family area. After a year, they would reevaluate the situation.

The father's threats had done no good; neither had the mother's pitiful pleading. The grandfather's plan gave the boy the responsibility to make the decision, and the consequences of each option were clear. After he thought for a while, the boy chose the first option of limiting his time on the computer to two hours a day.

> *The grandfather's plan gave the boy the responsibility to make the decision, and the consequences of each option were clear.*

The grandfather also had a private talk with the parents, and he told them they would have to change just as much as the boy. He told the father to quit threatening, and instead to give his son choices and consequences. He told the boy's mother that pity isn't love. If she continued to treat him as a baby, he would continue to act like one, but if she treated him like a responsible young man, he would probably grow into that identity.

As the weeks went by, the young man tested his parents a time or two by staying on the computer longer than his allotted two hours. In response, his father calmly told him he would not be allowed to play on it the next day. His mother instinctively wanted to change her husband's mind, but as soon as she realized what she was doing, she backed her husband's decision. The boy's grades improved, he gained new self-respect because he made his own decisions, and—perhaps most important for the long-term health of the family— the parents learned a new way of relating to their son. This grandfather used a simple skill of clarifying choices and consequences, gave authority to the boy to make his own decision, and taught the parents to treat him like a responsible young man. All in a day's work for a wise granddad!

The next chapter shows how your life's story, your legacy, can have a powerful, positive impact on your grandchildren.

REFLECTION

1. Why do you think children contact their grandparents after experiencing catastrophes?

2. What is the contribution of television, commercials, and technology in promising an easy, exciting life to young people? Cite some examples.

Describe the impact these promises have had on you and your grandchildren.

3. What are some specific ways to encourage the following young people?

. . . Someone who is tempted to give in to peer pressure.

. . . Someone who is tempted to give up.

. . . Someone who is tempted to lash out.

. . . Someone who is tempted to look for the easy way.

4. Describe "The Stockdale Paradox."

5. What are some ways you can tell if helping someone is actually hurting him?

6. Have you seen triangles used in your family to create confusion and win allegiance? Explain.

7. Think of the last two or three problems your grandchildren experienced. List several possible options that would help them clarify choices in each case.

Describe some possible consequences for each one.

8. In summary, what are some specific things you can do to impart courage to your grandchild?

How can you help your grandchild overcome self-pity and learned helplessness?

The Connection Principle: Leaving a Legacy

"The family is our refuge and springboard; nourished on it, we can advance to new horizons. In every conceivable manner, the family is link to our past, bridge to our future."
—*Alex Haley, author of* Roots

*E*very person inherently asks three crucial questions: Where did I come from? Why am I here? And where am I going? As Alex Haley's comment indicates, the family helps us answer those questions in a way that gives us stability and hope. If a child discovers he has a heritage he can be proud of, that story will be a springboard for his future. Of course, every family has its black sheep. For every great-great-grandfather who won medals fighting for our country, we can uncover a distant (or not-too-distant) uncle who was put in prison for stealing. All families are checkered with the good and the bad. Children can learn from all those stories, even the most painful and shameful ones.

In many cases, children are powerfully affected by the stories they learn from their grandparents. In my early years, I was fascinated by my great-grandfather, even though I only got to see him once, and that was when I was a six-week-old baby. Yet from the time I was a small boy, I heard stories about him from family and friends. My middle name, Lee, was in his honor. He had been a minister, and later when I went into the ministry, older adults often told me that I reminded them of him.

Because everyone spoke of him with so much respect and appreciation, I pored over family records to find out more about him. I talked to people who had known him. I discovered that in the rural area where he lived, he was a hero because of his generosity and kindness to so many people. Today, only one portrait hangs in my office: It is a pencil and charcoal drawing of my great-grandfather. Every day I'm aware that, in a sense, this venerable man is watching me, and I want to live up to his example. His life is a powerful part of my identity as a man and as a minister.

> *Every day I'm aware that, in a sense, this venerable man is watching me, and I want to live up to his example.*

Another great-grandfather was in the cattle business, and he was no less influential. He passed along his knowledge of ranching, and today some of our family members still raise cattle.

TWO LIVES, TWO LEGACIES

My mother's two grandfathers were very different men from vastly different circumstances. Her father's father, Mack Keenum, grew up in abject poverty. In fact, even the poor people thought he was poor. But he worked hard to raise the standard of living for himself and his family. He is considered one of the great success stories of our family. My mother's other grandfather,

John Wesley Bynum, was from a wealthy family. In the old South, he would have been called "landed," which means he and his family owned a lot of land. Though he had so many resources, his legacy is cast in darker shades. He left his wife and children for another woman, and that was back at the turn of the century when society considered such behavior utterly reprehensible. Both men left a legacy, one of hard work and integrity, the other of pain caused by selfishness and foolish decisions. I learned lessons from both of them, and I hope my children will learn valuable lessons from both the good and the bad examples in our family history.

Much of what I knew about John Wesley Bynum, my wealthy but wayward great-grandfather, came from vivid stories my grandmother told me as a boy. She explained that he was a brilliant businessman with a gift for making money. He had built one of the nicest homes in that part of the state and was revered by all, but after the divorce his reputation was shattered and his land was divided. My grandmother (and her sisters) told me that when he had the affair with the other woman, he became abusive toward his wife, their mother. My grandmother was the only one in the family who maintained a relationship with her father, but her perception was clear. She often remarked, "Son, that's what can happen when success goes to your head. Pride will ruin you and lead you to make foolish decisions." Today, John Wesley Bynum is buried in a cemetery not far from where our family lives, but no other family members are buried near him. Even in his death, his foolishness has isolated him.

Not many years ago, my mother's brother wondered if all those stories about John Wesley Bynum were true, so he looked up the divorce documents in the county archives. The official records indicate that his abuse may have been even worse than my great-grandmother ever told family members.

In stark contrast, my mother's other grandfather, Mack Keenum, was so illiterate that he never even signed his name the same way twice, but he built a strong family that perpetuated love and strength for generations. His children enjoyed stable families with lots of love. They, like their father, were far from rich in terms of land, possessions, and money in the bank, but they were fabulously rich in the things that really count. I thank my grandmother for telling me stories about both great-grandfathers, because both examples can teach a young man valuable lessons.

My father also had two grandparents who were diametrically different. One, Lee Waldrep, was a gentle man who was in the ministry. His impact was quiet but powerful. The other grandfather was a hard living, loud, cursing, drinking, strongly opinionated man who was feared more than loved. But in his later years, my great-grandfather, Earnest Terry, found Christ and his life was radically changed. He learned to treat people with kindness instead of intimidation. The legacy he left behind when he died was proof that no matter how hard-hearted you have been, you can change.

As my grandmothers told me those stories about my four great-grandfathers, I have seen myself in all of them. Two of them compel me to be a better person and to leave a legacy of hope and love, and two of them remind me what I could easily become if pride, cursing, drinking or any other foolishness were to take root in my life. I learn from one that a single foolish choice can ruin a life and a family, but I learn from another that no matter how many mistakes a person makes, positive change is still possible. All of these form my family's legacy that is passed to my daughters, and later will be passed along to their kids.

A single person can have a powerful impact on generations to follow—for good or ill. For example, a study of the descendants of Jonathan Edwards, one of the leaders of the Great Awakening in early 18th-century America, is revealing. Among his descendants are presidents of eight colleges, about 100 college professors, 100 preachers and missionaries, more than 100 lawyers, 60 physicians, 30 judges, 60 prominent authors, 25 officers in the army and navy, and 80 holders of important public offices, including three United States senators and a Vice President.[13]

Another man from the same era shows, in contrast, how a single person can influence his family legacy in a negative way. Max Jukes was a petty thief who had 310 descendants who died as paupers, 150 criminals, 100 drunkards, and seven convicted of murder. More than half of the women in Jukes' lineage were prostitutes.

Grandparents have a powerful impact on generations to come. Mine have been far more like Jonathan Edwards than Max Jukes. I hope yours are too!

---

13 Edith A. Winship, *The Human Legacy of Jonathan Edwards,* (The World's Work, October, 1903).

DON'T USE YOUR STORY TO SHAME OTHERS

Some of us use our personal histories to correct and shame a whining child. A grandchild may complain, "I don't have time to get my homework done," and we jump right in with the same old clichés: "Well, when I was your age, I had to get up at five in the morning to feed the chickens, milk the cows, and clean the barn. Then I had to walk five miles to school—uphill. We didn't have computers in those days, no sir. We had slate boards and chalk. And we had to memorize Latin and study Greek history. We didn't watch movies all day and have recess every time we turned around. And after I walked home—uphill again—I had to pick cotton and help Mama cook supper. If you think you don't have time to do homework, think again! You should be ashamed of yourself for complaining like that!"

> *"If you think you don't have time to do homework, think again! You should be ashamed of yourself for complaining like that!"*

Have you heard grandparents talk to kids like that? I sure have, and it hasn't had the impact the grandparents desired. Instead of shaming them, it is much preferable to identify with them. You can say, "I felt that way when this or that happened in my life." If you identify with them without correcting them, they are much more likely to ask, "Well, what did you do about it?" At that point, you can share a similar experience without lecturing or demanding anything from the child. If the child is listening, he will "connect the dots" and make a relevant application, or he will ask you for advice. Even then, be careful not to make his decision for him. Clarify choices and consequences, but don't demand compliance. Let him make his own choices and experience the consequences, good or bad.

BE HONEST, BE APPROPRIATE

Every story, no matter how glorious or how sordid, can be a valuable lesson to help shape a young life. Be honest about your joys and trials. Grandchildren will appreciate your candor about family successes and struggles, but also be appropriate. Gauge the level of details to fit the developmental age of the child. For example, you don't need to tell grade-school children the gruesome details of violence between family members, but as they mature, more revelation is appropriate. The fact of a divorce may be inescapable, but you don't necessarily need to tell a six-year-old child about the adultery that caused the breakup. Crimes, sexual activities, and violence are sensitive topics for young minds. You can always tell children more later, but once something is out of your mouth, it is gone for good. As the old saying goes, "You can't unring a bell."

In addition, consider withholding information about anyone who is still alive and has changed. For example, you may not want to talk about a brother's crime committed 30 years ago if he learned from his mistake and has lived an exemplary life since then. If your brother wants to talk about it so that the younger generation will learn from his mistake and his example of repentance, that's fine. But it's for him to tell, not you.

Telling his story without his permission may wound him unnecessarily, and it betrays his trust in you.

A friend of mine had a grandfather who was known as a fun-loving but hot-tempered man. When the friend was a boy, his mother told him lots of stories about his grandfather. Many were quite humorous, like when he had won a dance contest he entered under the name of someone who couldn't dance at all, and the other guy's name was in all the newspapers as the best dancer in the area! But later, my friend's mother began telling other stories about her dad. My friend learned that his grandfather had killed a man but was never arrested for the crime, and that he had committed other acts of violence on respected members of the community. As his mother told these stories, her face reflected the shame and heartache caused by her father's outbursts of rage. Her family had lost respect from those who knew about the incidents. My friend had learned early that violence causes incredible shame and pain, both at the moment it occurs and possibly for many more years to come. That is a valuable lesson for a young man to learn.

As his mother told these stories, her face reflected the shame and heartache caused by her father's outbursts of rage.

STUPID MISTAKES, GLORIOUS VICTORIES

Young people can learn from everything that has happened in our lives and in our family history, whether stupid mistakes or glorious victories. They need to hear stories about when we did the right thing but weren't rewarded for it. They need to hear that doing right is the right thing to do, even when the consequences are unfair. Today, children face moral complexities at school, in sports, and at home.

In one situation, a young girl and three of her friends cheated on a test. The teacher suspected them and asked them to admit they had cheated. The girl told the truth and apologized, "Yes, ma'am. I'm sorry I cheated." She was punished with three days of detention. But when the other girls were brought in, they denied they had cheated. The teacher had no hard evidence, so she had to let them go. The girl who admitted she had cheated got punished while the others got off scot-free—at least for now. This little girl could use a good story from a grandparent about the benefits (and the pains) of being honest even if nobody else is.

A grandparent can help the child understand that life can be confusing and unfair, but ultimately, doing the right thing produces genuine blessings. In the little girl's eyes, her friends got away with their crime. But a wise grandparent can tell stories of how "getting away" with something today makes it easier and more attractive to keep cheating, and if that pattern persists, how the person drifts down a long and dangerous path, becoming insensitive to right and wrong.

Many times, major tragedies are the result of a string of smaller, foolish decisions that weren't directly and immediately linked to painful consequences. Many of those who steal from an employer, cheat on a spouse, or lie to their friends are those who "got away with" lesser indiscretions when they were young. A grandchild needs to hear stories about those who did right and those who did wrong, and the eventual consequences of each.

Some Christians believe and teach that God will right every wrong and bless every good deed—today! That may be how we want life to be, but it simply isn't the way it works. Yes, someday God will bring all events into the light of His judgment, but that may be a long time off. In the meantime, we sometimes find good being ignored or punished, and evil being rewarded. The psalmist wrote of this reality in Psalm 73, and Solomon described the phenomenon in Ecclesiastes. The wisdom of a grandparent may be the only source of insight for a confused grandchild who experiences injustice at school, in the neighborhood, or at home. The reward is not that justice is meted out at the very moment an unfair act is committed, but that in the long run, doing right leaves us with a clear conscience. And a clear conscience is worth more than gold.

Another lesson grandparents can impart is that sometimes the thing we want so desperately today is the very thing that can ruin our lives tomorrow. I am reminded of a story about a visitor to a state mental institution. He walked down the hall and heard a man weeping and calling out over and over again, "Mary! Mary! Mary!"

The visitor was moved by the obvious distress in the man's voice. He asked, "What happened to this man, and who's Mary?"

A nurse told him, "He was in love with a woman years ago, but she refused to marry him. Her rejection drove him insane."

The visitor walked down the hall where he heard a second man's voice. This man, too, was weeping and wailing, calling out, "Mary! Mary! Mary!"

The visitor turned to the nurse and asked, "And what happened to *him?*"

The nurse replied, "He's the one who married Mary."

The moral of the story is that sometimes a most disappointing turn of events is the very thing that secures a better future for us. Most grandparents can provide numerous examples of this truth.

As you tell your family's story, paint a clear picture of the consequences of people's decisions. A young woman may have been desperately in love, only to get pregnant and have to marry someone who really didn't love her much. Her consequence of a moment of delight is a lifetime of heartache. Foolish decisions about money can have an impact on the individual, the welfare of the immediate family, and the reputation of descendants for years to come.

Bitterness can ruin a family just as much as a gun, a baby, or a jail cell. Sadly, bitterness is perhaps the most common legacy in families, and it leaves devastating consequences. The passion to get revenge gives people energy and keeps them awake at night as they plot how to punish someone who has hurt them. But they waste their time and energy on the fruitless pursuit, and eventually it consumes them in depression, psychosomatic illnesses, and strained or broken relationships.

> *Sadly, bitterness is perhaps the most common legacy in families, and it leaves devastating consequences.*

USING STORIES TO TEACH

Doyle Combs was a man who was like a grandfather to me. In fact, he and his wife were seated as grandparents at our wedding. Doyle often came to hear me speak when I was a young minister. I tried hard back then, but in my zeal, I said some things that confused people and did some things that didn't help my ministry much. When I made a dumb mistake, Doyle never came right up and said, "Phil, you said something stupid a few minutes ago." Instead, he waited a day or so, and then he called or came by to see me. In an offhanded way, he would begin with a chuckle followed by a story about his own experience when he was young in the ministry—a story that was close enough to my own mistake that I couldn't miss the point.

If I had made fun of fat people in my message, Doyle would tell me, "I told a story about cross-eyed people, and you know what, there was a cross-eyed man sitting there listening to me. Can you imagine how he felt? I hope I never make fun of anybody like that again." Doyle didn't lecture me, he didn't blame me, and he didn't threaten me. He just told me a story about his own life. He let me make the connection. I always appreciated not only his insight, but also his kindness in how he taught me.

I learned valuable lessons from Doyle's graceful examples, and I grew closer to him. Those are the marks of a great communicator. It is easy to get a point across if we don't care how much we hurt someone, or we can err on the other extreme and be so gentle that we don't make the point at all. Doyle found the right blend of grace and truth.

BE PREPARED, BE SPONTANEOUS

I believe many grandparents miss wonderful opportunities to tell their stories to their grandchildren because they aren't prepared. The events of today crowd our memories out of our minds, and we may believe nobody is interested in the past anyway. Yet young people are usually fascinated by accounts of hardship and victories—if they are told with enthusiasm and enough detail to make the story come alive.

Listen carefully to people who are great storytellers. Learn from them. They move the saga along with clear descriptions of the events and people's reactions. They paint vivid word pictures of green meadows, towering mountains, crashing storms, and quiet streams. They grimace when they talk of pain, and they laugh when they tell of great joy. Become an expert at telling your own story so that you thoroughly enjoy it. If you enjoy it, others probably will too. (In the appendix of this book you will find an outline and worksheet to help you construct your story.)

One reason some of us get negative feedback from our families is that we tell the same stories over and over again. Even great stories lose their punch if they are told too often. Don't feel that you have to tell your story every time you see your grandchild. It will have more meaning if you are selective in the timing, the length, and the way you tell your stories.

If you need to broaden your storytelling repertoire, take time to consider other aspects of your life that may be just as interesting, but have been neglected up to now. Some of us focus on a particularly difficult time, and we forget to tell about all the wonderful times. Conversely, some of us feel so uncomfortable about past pain that we become afraid to share anything that reminds us of those moments.

We may plan to tell our stories at a given place and time, like a reunion or Sunday dinner, but spontaneous opportunities are often the most teachable moments. As you drive your granddaughter to the mall to go shopping, tap into your memory banks and tell stories that relate to that activity. ("I remember when my grandmother took me shopping for. . . .") When you're out on a boat fishing with your grandson, talk about when your dad caught the biggest catfish anybody had ever seen—just before he fell in the lake!

Share your stories and your feelings without demanding any response. You will always be a better teacher when you have a willing student, so build an atmosphere of trust and love. As you tell part of your story, you might pause to ask, "Do you ever feel that way?" or, "Has anything like that ever happened to you?"

If you live a long way from your grandchild, take time to think and pray before you talk on the phone.

Connecting with your grandchild takes time and energy. Close proximity certainly is a benefit, but it isn't a necessity. If you live a long way from your grandchild, take time to think and pray before you talk on the phone. Consider how you might connect beneath the surface. If you find out he's having a particular problem or is experiencing a great victory, take time to explore it together. If you don't have time to share your story at that moment, call back in a day or two. He will appreciate the special attention.

I encourage you to put your story in a form that can be passed down from generation to generation. You might want to write it, produce an audiotape, or make a video. Your grandchildren will be so grateful to have it when you've finished. Again, make sure you tell the story with colorful details and enthusiasm. Some people prefer to be interviewed by someone who knows enough of the story to prod their memory, press for more detail, or keep things moving if they get bogged down a bit.

A LEGACY OF GIFTS

Some grandparents make quite an effort to leave a legacy of gifts to their grandkids. I know one grandmother who saved her money and got each of her grandchildren a beautiful watch with a lovely inscription on the back, and another who made a quilt for each grandchild. A grandfather I know made wooden toys that could be passed along from generation to generation.

Of course, many grandparents leave wills to designate specific things for each person in the family. Too often, though, a young person who receives a bed or painting sees it as just another piece of old furniture and doesn't understand how the grandparent might have treasured it. If you are planning to leave items to people in your family, tell them ahead of time and explain the significance of the item to you. And do what you can to minimize jealousy among those receiving things from you.

One grandmother left a ring to her teenage grand-daughter after explaining she had received it from her husband when she was 25, during a time when they had very little money. Her husband had worked nights and weekends for months to pay for the ring, and when he gave it to her, both of them cried because they loved each other so much. It wasn't a spectacular ring that would be featured by Tiffany or Cartier, but the story behind it gave it more value than any ring in any store in the world. The teenager understood the depth of love behind the gift, and she treasured it for the rest of her life. When she is older, she will pass it along to her daughter or granddaughter, and she'll be careful to explain what a poor young man did to show his great love to his darling wife.

In the next chapter, we will examine how to build moral character into the life of a grandchild.

REFLECTION

1. What are some of the stories of victory passed down in your family?

How have these shaped your own life?

2. What are some of the stories of heartache or failure in your family history?

    Have these stories been used to teach moral lessons, or have they been only sources of shame? Explain.

3. What are some ways grandparents shame their grandkids with their stories?

    Why do you think they do that?

4. For your stories involving vivid realities about the past, what limitations should you make when talking to grade school children?

What would you keep from junior highers?

What, if anything, would you withhold from high schoolers?

5. Which parts of your story have "connected" best with your grandchildren? Was the connection planned or spontaneous? Explain.

6. Think of the particular stresses each of your grand-children face today. What are some ways you can use parts of your story to teach them, like Doyle did with me?

7. How might you use gifts as part of your legacy? How can you make these as meaningful as possible?

8. Would it be wise and good for you to write or tape your story for posterity? What do you need to do to make that happen? (See the appendix for an outline of how to prepare your story.)

CHAPTER 8

The Conviction Principle: Developing Moral Tenacity

🌸

"The time came when the beliefs in which I was once brought up and which, in fact, had given my life direction even while my intellect still challenged their validity, were recognized by me as mine in their own right and by my free choice."
—Dag Hammarskjold

A friend of mine has a daughter who is a Resident Assistant in a dorm at the University of Texas. She and the other RAs were taught that the highest virtue of leadership is tolerance, that is, the unquestioned acceptance of every lifestyle. For example, homosexuality and bisexuality were presented as perfectly acceptable lifestyles, and the RAs were told that if they cast aspersions on people of these persuasions, or, heaven forbid, they tried to change these people, they would be in violation of campus policy.

At one point in the training, the leader told all the RAs to stand at one end of a large room while he stood at the other end. He yelled to them, "The distance between you and me is the difference between intolerance, on the wall behind you, and tolerance on this wall behind me. That wall represents rigid absolutes. This wall represents the acceptance and love for all people. I want you to stand at the point in the room that demonstrates where you are between those two walls.

Some of the RAs took a few steps and remained somewhat close to the tolerance wall; some gravitated to the middle of the room; and many didn't stop until they were standing next to the leader. But everyone moved—except for my friend's daughter, who stayed right where she was next to the wall of absolutes. The rest of the people in the room looked at her with various degrees of self-righteous indignation. A few mumbled under their breath, but she held firm in her convictions that God has established a standard for right and wrong.

THE EROSION OF ABSOLUTES

In an attempt to right past wrongs of rigid prejudice, "tolerance" has actually come to refer (for many people) to the promotion of lifestyles that have been considered shameful by most societies since moral codes were developed. Being "judgmental" of people with such lifestyles is considered the worst possible sin. Scorn is heaped on people who define morality too rigidly, such as those who hold to a traditional Judeo-Christian perspective. Therefore, in essence, tolerance is extended only to those who espouse formerly aberrant, yet now acceptable, lifestyles.

Certainly we should love all people, but loving them doesn't mean we accept—and even applaud—behavior that God has said is wrong.

Certainly we should love all people, but loving them doesn't mean we accept—and even applaud—behavior that God has said is wrong. If you think this kind of teaching and peer pressure happens only at the

University of Texas, think again. Teaching tolerance has become the norm in schools, from grade school to colleges, throughout our land.

Of course, most of us grew up believing that tolerance is a good thing. When we hear how the term is being used today, some of us scratch our heads. Our mothers told us to be nice to people who were different than us, to "tolerate" them. She wanted us to be patient with difficult people and kind to those who are suffering. But today the world has a far different definition of "tolerance." The word is pregnant with a moral philosophy that there are no absolutes; experience determines what is good. People have a God-given thirst for truth and justice, but today, the message is, "If it seems right for you, then go for it." When objective truth is discarded, people are left to determine their own values based on whatever standards they choose.

How did this happen? How did our society, once based on strong, clear, Judeo-Christian values, disintegrate into the mush of tolerance? It didn't happen quickly. Some historians point to the Age of Enlightenment as a significant first step in this long slide away from absolutes. In his book, *Generating Hope,* Jimmy Long comments on philosopher René Descartes' desire to strengthen his faith in Christ by using human wisdom. Long reports, "To accomplish this task, Descartes developed the principle of doubt through the use of human reason. From this beginning he coined the phrase, 'I think, therefore I am.' He believed self-knowledge was the foundation on which all knowledge could be built. As a result, human reason usurped God as the basis for all knowledge. What I think, not what God reveals, becomes the measure of truth."[14]

German theologians embraced a similar perspective in the late 19th century. To counter this drift from biblical truth, a movement to uphold the Scriptures was established, a movement called "fundamentalism." Today fundamentalism has a reputation in the secular media for being blind, rigid, and uncaring, but its roots are the defense of the truth of God that opposes the moral erosion caused by relativism.

As we saw in an earlier chapter, we can trace the recent decline of moral absolutes by looking at popular culture. The World War II generation fought against Nazi aggression and Japanese imperialism. The lines between good and evil were clear in that conflict. Their Boomer children, however, experienced the uncertainty of the Cold War, the possibility of nuclear annihilation, the social upheaval of the Civil Rights Movement, and the lack of purpose and resolve in the Vietnam conflict. Boomers reacted to the instability of their times by experimenting with drugs and sex in a genuine cultural revolution. As a generation, the insecure Boomers proved to be too self-absorbed to be good parents, and many of their children, the Busters, became "latchkey kids" with no clear direction, no clear values, and no clear grasp of right and wrong.

In this vacuum, Busters turned even more to personal experience as their standard for decision-making. In his book, *The Invisible Generation*, George Barna observed,

---

14 Jimmy Long, *Generating Hope*, (Intervarsity Press, Downers Grove, Illinois, 1997), p. 62.

"70% [of Busters] claim that absolute does not exist, that all truth is relative and personal. . . . Two-thirds of the [Buster] generation concede that 'nothing can be known for certain except the things that you experience in your own life.' "[15] It was only a small step from this Buster relativism to the RA training on tolerance at the University of Texas. In today's youth culture, those who promote absolute truth are thought to be old fashioned, out-of-touch, narrow, rigid, and in a word, *intolerant.*

CONVICTIONS AND PREFERENCE

Grandparents tend to have convictions, while parents and grandchildren have only preferences. A conviction is something a person stands by, no matter what the consequences may be, but a preference can change with the wind. A person who has firm convictions will hold to his beliefs even if he loses his job and his friends, even if it costs him money or his reputation. He won't steal or lie to get what he wants. A person whose moral foundation is built on the sands of preference, however, might choose to tell the truth if it is convenient, but he will lie if that better serves his immediate purposes. He prefers to be honest, but not at any price. Conviction reflects character "in the dark" when nobody sees what you are doing, but

A person who has firm convictions will hold to his beliefs even if he loses his job and his friends, even if it costs him money or his reputation.

---

15 George Barna, *The Invisible Generation,* (Barna Research Group, Glendale, California, 1992), p. 81.

preference encourages you to do the right thing only if people are watching.

Many of today's young people live in an environment of preference. At home, parents make moral choices based on what suits them at the time. Children see the inconsistencies. The father says he supports the government and respects the law, but he uses a radar detector in his car to avoid speeding tickets. He expects people to pay him back whatever they owe him, but he tries to get out of paying his own debts. The mother buys a dress and wears it that night, then the next day she takes it back to the store and says she needs to return it because it doesn't fit. The family goes to a restaurant where "Kids under 12 eat free." The dad tells the waitress that his 14-year-old is only 11, and he justifies it to the child by saying, "You don't eat any more than an 11-year-old."

At school, friends cheat if it gets them a better grade without having to go to the trouble of studying. Some are involved in premarital sex, and they shrug and say, "So what? Nobody is being hurt, and it makes us happy." Students flatter teachers to their faces, and ridicule them behind their backs.

People have always made bad choices. The problem these days is that more people are doing it, and they are making those bad choices with very little guilt and remorse. Sin seems right and natural, and that's the real problem.

Grandparents need to model clear, compelling convictions by living up to what they say is important, not changing their values to fit each situation. When they take a grandchild to a restaurant and the waiter says, "It looks like this girl gets to eat free tonight," the grandparent can say, "No, she's actually 14. We'll be happy to pay for her to eat with us." No hesitation, no question, no grumbling—just the conviction to do what is right no matter what the cost.

EXPLAIN THE WHYS

In countless situations when grandparents have the choice to fudge the truth or abide by it, they can use those opportunities to explain the underlying reasons for their decision. The combination of modeling the right choice and explaining the rationale can shape a young life. Look for these opportunities, and use them to teach the following benefits of doing the right thing:

The benefit of a clear conscience

One of the most valuable character qualities a person can possess is a sensitive heart. A finely tuned conscience pricks the heart of a person who has done wrong. Ignoring that inner voice numbs him and eventually erodes his conscience so that it no longer affirms right and challenges wrong. After making a tough but honorable decision, a grandparent can say, "I know my decision cost me something, but I did the right thing. Now I can sleep well tonight."

After making a tough but honorable decision, a grandparent can say, "I know my decision cost me something, but I did the right thing. Now I can sleep well tonight."

The benefit of avoiding death

The Bible says, "The wages of sin is death" (Rom 6:23). When we do wrong, something in us dies: our integrity, our character, our trustworthiness, or a bit of our hearts. We usually don't notice a dramatic difference after a single incident, but the cumulative effect works much like starvation. Missing one meal doesn't affect a person much, but after not eating for a while, he becomes weak, gaunt, and more susceptible to diseases. If he doesn't reverse the trend, he will die. In the same way, a person who starves himself morally becomes weak, susceptible to temptations and vices of every kind, and spiritually and morally emaciated.

The benefit of being trustworthy

As a person demonstrates quiet conviction, doing the right thing without bragging about it, others sit up and notice. Who are those in any field of life who are considered trustworthy? They are the ones who have done the right thing time after time, no matter what price they have had to pay. A good reputation is built over years of consistently demonstrating, not just talking about, good and godly principles.

The benefit of eventual rewards

We may or may not be rewarded for doing the right thing today, but someday all our deeds will come to light and every good and honorable act will be rewarded. We are not promised that our rewards will all come in this life. Of those that do, some will come quickly and some will come years later. But we can be sure that someday we will be further rewarded for doing right—even if nobody but God saw what we have done. This encouragement may not hold much water for a person who wants immediate gratification, but a wise grandparent will teach the significance of this truth, and will demonstrate calm confidence in a sovereign, loving, and just God.

RESPECT FOR AUTHORITY

No institution can exist without respect for its authority. Schools, homes, companies, government, clubs, teams, and other groups can function only as well as the respect shown by those within the organization. The vast majority of older grandparents understand the significance of respect for authority. When they were young, in their generation of clear right and wrong, their watchword was *duty*. People put the needs of others above themselves. They gladly sacrificed to protect their country and provide for their families. Relationships in the community were based on the common good, not selfish gain. During the social upheaval of the radical 60s, however, the goal changed from duty to *rights*. People became self-focused and demanded their own needs be met even if others had to suffer.

Many young people today have watched parents focus on their own needs, and the result has been failed marriages, shattered families, and misplaced purposes. In this confusion, these young people sense a genuine desire for direction and moral clarity, but they are left with only the path of experience, not moral truth, to take them there. They aren't angry at authority like the young people of the 60s, and they don't feel abandoned by authority like the young people of the 80s, but they don't quite feel connected to authority today. They are still asking, "What really matters?" The answer has traditionally come from authority figures, and they have none they really trust.

Grandparents can step into this vacuum and model a life of passion for a purpose bigger than themselves. They can overflow with drive and determination to accomplish things that really matter. They will serve instead of demanding to be served, and they will give instead of demanding that others first meet their needs. In short, they will joyfully do their duty and experience great fulfillment in doing it. This example will also demonstrate proper respect for every organization—not blind adherence, but genuine respect—with eyes open, willing to accept the good while trying to change the bad, and without bailing out on marriage, the government, or the church.

> *Grandparents can step into this vacuum and model a life of passion for a purpose bigger than themselves. They can overflow with drive and determination to accomplish things that really matter.*

ACCEPT PEOPLE UNCONDITIONALLY

As we take our eyes off our own rights and our own needs, we return to the conviction that every person is valuable—the corporate executive and the bum on the street, the fashion model and the desperately poor single mother of four. We are all equal in the sense that we are all needy in the sight of God, and we are all valuable in His eyes. This conviction of the innate value of each person encourages us to love everyone unconditionally. When we value one person over another, we make a judgment God does not make.

Prejudice and preference, be it racial, ethnic, or economic, is an attempt to raise oneself at another's expense. In past generations, prejudice was largely seen in relationships between blacks and whites, and it was legalized in housing, restaurants, and many other parts of society. Today, legalized prejudice has been rescinded, and our culture is more of a melting pot than ever before.

But preference and the air of superiority are just as real as ever. Preference is based more on economics than ethnicity. People are judged not by their skin color, but by the brand name on their fashion jeans.

A friend of mine vividly recalls the day his high school was integrated. He told me, "I never thought I was prejudiced at all. My father was good to the black people who worked for him, but of course, that was as far as it went. We certainly never had any black people over for a meal when I was a boy, and to be honest, I don't have many black 'friends' today. My son, though, is a college student with good friends who are Asian, Mexican, Peruvian, Nigerian, and from many other countries. One day as we were talking about his friends, he said, 'Dad, you're prejudiced.' I told him emphatically that I'm not, but he pointed out some things I'd just said that revealed some attitudes I had. And he was right. I never saw myself as prejudiced, but I was looking at how far I'd come, not how far I needed to go."

My friend had a new insight about the insidious nature of prejudice because he listened to his son. The schools I attended were integrated a year or two before I started the first grade, so I never attended a segregated school. In addition, when I was young my father operated a business where two African-American men were not only employees, but also my father's friends. They came to our home many times when I was a boy, so I grew up without the environment of prejudice that many other people experienced.

My children may not point out my errors and sins of prejudice, but I have made errors and committed sins in other areas of my life. When they point out my inconsistencies, I shouldn't disregard them or blow them off in any way. Instead, I need to say, "You're right. I was wrong when I said that or did that." An adult's example of honesty and contrition is tremendously valuable in shaping a young person's humility and helping him or her learn to be open to the Lord's reproof and correction.

We will accept people only if we feel loved and secure ourselves. Otherwise, we tend to feel threatened when someone wears different clothes, talks with a different accent, or has a different skin color. In fact, we will only accept others to the extent that we feel accepted ourselves. The Bible describes this phenomenon in three passages:

- "Beloved, if God so loved us, we also ought to love one another" (I John 4:11);
- "And be kind to one another, tenderhearted, forgiving one another, just as God in Christ also forgave you" (Eph 4:32); and

- "Therefore receive [or accept] one another, just as Christ also received us, to the glory of God" (Rom 15:7).

Do you see the connection in these instructions? We are to love others just as Christ loves us, forgive them just as Christ has forgiven us, and accept them just as Christ has accepted us. We should set our goals to do no less. Our ability to *express* love, forgiveness, and acceptance to others is proportional to our own *experience* of these wonderful qualities.

Young people, by definition, are immature, passionate creatures. Adolescents struggle through one of the most insecure times in life, and they typically suffer from inferiority. They feel unloved, unforgiven, and unacceptable. Their peers are just as insecure, so they are little help. In fact, they frequently make a sport of putting each other down in the hope of feeling superior, if only for a moment.

A wise, loving grandparent can step into this whirlwind of insecurity and passion and calm the storm by imparting the love, forgiveness, and acceptance every child needs. Telling your story of your own struggles helps your grandchild identify with you. You can share how someone imparted love when you felt like no one would ever care about you, how someone forgave you after you hurt them, and how someone reached out to accept you when you felt alone. Even if you have no specific anecdotes, you can still communicate your empathy and be there for your grandchild.

Telling your story of how someone stepped into your life to accept you unconditionally is only part of your role. More importantly, you can be that person for your grandchild. At her most unlovely moment, you can embrace her. When she is most out of control, you can reach out to show you don't condemn her and you won't abandon her. When she has made tragically wrong decisions, don't stand aloof and look down your nose at her because you are embarrassed by her actions. Don't tell her she has ruined her life. Instead, forgive her. Extend the hand of grace and speak words of kindness, strength, and hope. She may resist at first because she doesn't feel she deserves anyone's love. That's natural and normal, but don't let it drive you away. Continue to show your love. Gradually, she will believe that your love is real, and just as important, that it is totally unconditional. As she soaks in that love, she will never be the same.

CONVICTION BASED ON FAITH

Genuine convictions are always based on something bigger than ourselves. As I have talked to thousands of grandparents across the country, many of them tell me that their convictions come directly from their faith in God and His Word. Their relationship with Christ has given them strength when they felt weak and direction when they were lost. The truth of the Scriptures has answered life's most fundamental questions about their identity and purpose.

The pages of the Bible tell us that we are tragically fallen, but deeply loved, completely forgiven, and totally accepted children of God. We now have a purpose to honor the One who bought us, who saved us from death, and who has given us a destiny to live with Him forever. No matter how much we do right, nothing can make God love us more, and no matter how much we have done wrong, nothing can cause Him to love us less. As we begin to comprehend His grace, we are motivated to live for Him every moment of every day.

We have said that young people today live in a culture that lacks moral absolutes and truth. Grandparents can impart the "faith of our fathers" to their grandchildren and watch as preference is replaced with conviction, confusion with purpose, and relativism with truth. Young people listen as you pray, and they watch as you live out your faith. As they see your consistency and sense your hope, they will want what you've got.

Grandparents can impart the "faith of our fathers" to their grandchildren and watch as preference is replaced with conviction, confusion with purpose, and relativism with truth.

Time after time, I've listened to men and women, young and old, tell me how a grandparent's faith shaped their lives. One lady, Joyce, told me that her grandparents had traveled from Tennessee to Alabama in a covered wagon near the turn of the century. They crossed the Tennessee River on a ferry, pulling themselves across with ropes. "To make a trip like that," Joyce reflected, "they must have been very patient and persistent. They were willing to work hard to provide for their family."

Joyce's grandparents had thirteen children and five grandchildren living in the same house with them when Joyce was a small child. Like countless other families during those desperate years, they had little to eat. But Joyce told me that her grandparents overflowed with hope and love: hope that someday their hard work and faithfulness would pay off, and love for every person around them. She told me they wanted her life to turn out better than theirs had. She said, "My grandparents and parents weren't educated, but they encouraged me to get a good education. They saw how hard they had to work to make a living, and they were determined that all of us would have better opportunities than they had."

Joyce spoke of how her grandparents had imparted clear values of loving people and being fair. "It was a small house," she recalled, "so we *had* to get along! We made our own toys and talked to each other for hours at a time. My grandparents couldn't afford much, but they made sure that whatever we wore was clean." Her grandparents put God first, and they allowed God's purpose and His will to shape every aspect of their lives.

As I talked to Joyce, she used one specific word several times. She said her grandparents were "positive" in their outlook on life, and they imparted optimism to every member of the family. They believed that God has an eternal purpose in every event in life. In the good times, He teaches us to be thankful, and in the difficult times, He builds our character and teaches us life's deepest lessons. That's a positive outlook!

Joyce told me that her grandparents didn't win the love and respect of the family by simply giving everybody whatever they wanted. She said, "If we wanted something, they told us to set a goal and work hard for it. That's what they did, and that's what they expected us to do. They sacrificed a lot to send us to school, but they didn't do things for us that we needed to do for ourselves."

Joyce's grandparents modeled a wonderful blend of grace and responsibility. They had a powerfully positive impact on the entire family by their outlook, their values, their example, and their faith. Joyce basked in her grandparents' presence, and they imparted to her the gift of spiritual life as they told her about Christ. "It was easy to believe that God loved me," she related, "because I saw God's love in their eyes and felt it in their hugs. And it was easy to believe that God had a good purpose for me because I saw them trust God through the good times and the bad. My Grandpa and Grandma didn't just talk about the Lord. His presence spilled out of their hearts every day."

What spills out of your heart every day? Is it the conviction that God is both good and great, gracious and sovereign over all of life? Or is it that He has let you down and He can't be trusted? Perhaps a grandparent's greatest legacy is passing along thankfulness, faith, and courage that come from a profound relationship with God. Such things can't be faked.

What spills out of your heart every day?

Convictions give us meaning, purpose, and direction. They answer life's biggest questions, and even when we are confused, they give us the confidence that God knows our situation and is in control. That confidence is a great gift to a child. That hope will carry him through the deepest struggles he will encounter, both today and for the rest of his life, long after his grandparents are gone. And ultimately, that is the legacy he will pass down to generations to come.

How can a grandparent impart faith? The demonstration of faith in action is perhaps the most powerful way. Whenever a grandparent makes choices shaped by his or her faith, a child will take notice. A grandchild will also notice if actions are not connected to the grandparent's words of faith, and the lack of consistency will have a damaging effect.

Make a connection between what you hear in the Sunday sermon and how you help your neighbor, between your prayer this morning and God's blessing this afternoon, between a promise in God's Word and a current difficulty you face. We demonstrate great faith when we continue to trust as our lives are stretched to the breaking point. In such difficult times, the courage to believe that God is good and sovereign may mean more to our grandchildren than in all the good times put together.

Conversations with a grandchild about spiritual things can be rich and rewarding for both of you. Simple statements show your grandchild how your faith is shaping your life, statements such as:

- "I was praying for you to do well on your test just this morning. How did it go?"
- "Let me show you a verse that I've been thinking about all day."
- "What did you think of the pastor's story about his friend and his dog?"

- "I wonder what the Lord wants me to do here."
- "A friend is having a very hard time right now. Let's stop and pray for her."

We've already talked about telling your family story, but don't forget to also tell your story of faith. Talk about how your faith was shaped by your parents and grandparents, the singular moments when God has seemed very near, and the struggles you have faced when He seemed far away. Tell your grandchildren about the people who encouraged you to trust God. Explain what was going on in your life at those important times and how God used those people to prod you along the journey of faith.

Be available to answer your grandchild's questions. Some may seem silly, such as, "Did my cat go to heaven when he died?" But even what you may consider silly questions can open the door for rich and warm discussions about God and eternal life. In a relationship with a child, no question is trivial. If you take time to answer them, your grandchild may come to you when death, disease, or despair challenges his view of God and his hope for the future.

"I had some very difficult years. I was far away from God, but I always knew my grandmother (or my grandfather) was praying for me."

I've talked to many men and women who have told me, "I had some very difficult years. I was far away from God, but I always knew my grandmother (or my grandfather) was praying for me. That confidence gave me a rope I could hold on to when life was out of control."

When we communicate to our grandchildren that we are praying for them, we are saying, "I love you enough to talk to God about you." If that grandchild gets involved in wrong behavior, knowing a grandparent is praying often gives him a reason to pause and think, "I shouldn't be doing this." We don't have to be eloquent in our prayers to be effective. A grandchild may only hear us pray at meals, but he knows we are praying consistently for him. If we tell him or write him a note to let him know we are praying specifically for him, he will remember, and our prayers will make a difference.

I've talked to men in prison, some of them hardened criminals, who have told me about their grandmother or grandfather's prayers. Those men have done some things that they are not proud of, and their only link to God (and hope) is the fact that they know their grandparents are praying for them.

Pray specifically for your grandchild's salvation, for growth and maturity, and for a hedge of protection. Examine the prayers of Paul as a model. Pray for a "spirit of wisdom and revelation of the knowledge of God," for strength, for purity of motives, and for your grandchild's joy in "knowing the love of Christ which passes knowledge." And pray that no hardship will be wasted. God will use every event in our lives, the good and the bad, to shape us, to deepen our dependence on Him, and to make us more useful for Him and His kingdom— if we will only trust Him. Ask God to give your grandchild the faith to believe that every difficulty has a purpose, and that every hardship is a steppingstone to know God better.

As we care for our grandchildren, we need to be careful not to step over the line into meddling. If we ask our friends to ask their grandchildren for information about ours, we are meddling. If we try to eavesdrop on their phone calls or "accidentally" find incriminating things in their rooms or backpacks, we have crossed over the line. Compulsive faultfinding isn't love, even if we try to justify it by claiming we do it for the child's own good so we can correct him or her.

The psalmist wrote, "Children are a heritage [or gift] from the Lord" (Psalm 127:3). By extension, your grand-children are also gifts from God, and we should treat valuable gifts with respect. When we suspect a grand-child is making self-destructive choices, we shouldn't sneak around to get information or find clues. Instead, we need to treat the child as a treasured, valuable gift and confront the issue directly and honestly.

Years ago, Debbie and I attended a conference where Gary Smalley spoke. His topic was the dynamics of mar-riage relationships, and at the beginning of his talk, he picked up a small velvet bag and took out a huge, sparkling gem. He told us, "I value the gem I hold in my hand at six million dollars, but if it ever gets a single flaw, the value will decrease dramatically." The audience of about a thousand people was very attentive as he contin-ued: "I want to teach you a lesson about trust. I'm going to give this gem to this lady in the front row. During the rest of my talk, I want you to pass it around from row to row so each person can hold it. Remember, if you drop it and it gets even the tiniest crack, the value will be, well, a lot less. Please don't drop it!"

Since Gary's talk was to be about trust, I assumed the passing of the gem was to show that he trusted us with his valuable gemstone. At the end of his presentation, someone returned the stone and Gary asked us, "When you passed the gem from one to another, did you handle it with great care, or did you just toss it to the next person?" Everybody laughed. Almost every person had used both hands to transfer the stone, and we had all been extremely careful. Then Gary held up the gem and told us, "Ladies and gentlemen, I want to let you in on a secret. This is just a piece of cut glass. It's not a gem at all. You can buy this for $10. You may say, 'Hey, wait a minute. You said it was worth six million dollars.' But I didn't say that. I said, 'I value it at six million dollars.' My point is that the way we treat something—or someone—is directly related to how much we value it. If we value a spouse highly, we will treat that person with great care and respect. But if we see that person as worthless, we will be rude, uncaring, and heartless."

What Gary wanted to teach about love between spouses, I want to apply to grandparents and their grandchildren. In that crowded room, I understood what it means to value people as gifts from the Lord. We don't handle diamonds the same way we handle pennies. If we lose a penny, we don't give it a second thought, but if we lose a diamond ring, we search everywhere until we find it. We need to see each person—spouse, child, or grandchild—as an incredibly valuable gift from the Lord.

Another person's value should never be based on his performance. When we value people only when they perform well and make us happy, we engender fear of failure, not security. When we smile only when someone accomplishes the goals we have set for him or her, we promote competition among those who strive to please us. That's not grace, and it certainly isn't unconditional love.

When we value people only when they perform well and make us happy, we engender fear of failure, not security.

God valued us so much that He gave His own Son as a sacrifice to buy us back from sin and destruction—and that was "while we were still sinners." We were hostile, enemies of God, alienated from Him, but He gave Himself for us anyway. That's the measure of God's love and how much He values us, and that's the example for us to follow as we value our grandchildren and show love to them.

My good friend Junior Hill has taught me a lot about loving people unconditionally. He said, "Suppose you and your spouse found out you are expecting identical twins. You would be so excited! But on the day of their birth, the doctor tells you, 'We had some complications after your first son was born. Your second son has experienced some brain damage. I'm so sorry.' You would love those two boys just the same, though their performance would be worlds apart. Now, fast-forward about 22 years. The first son has come home from graduation at Harvard University. He shows you a plaque that says he has graduated with the highest grades in the history of that prestigious university, and your eyes stream with tears of pride and joy. A few seconds later, your mentally challenged son tugs on your shirt. He exclaims, 'Look, Dad! I tied my shoes!' He has been try-ing to learn to tie his shoes for years, and he has finally accomplished it. You will hug him just as tight as you hugged the honor graduate, and your eyes will fill just as much with tears of joy. Their performance may be worlds apart, but your love is just the same."

Be careful to avoid dispensing love and affection for your grandchild as a reward for performing well or making you happy. Choose to love him or her no matter what. Put your arm around that dear, treasured grand-son or granddaughter and say, "I am so glad you are mine." End the sentence there. Don't add any condition-al "because" phrase. Just show your joy that this child is your beloved grandchild.

Your grandchild, like all of us, desperately needs unconditional love. God loves unconditionally, and if we are rightly related to God, so can we. We must learn to allow His kindness and compassion to overflow from our hearts. In fact, one of the primary means God uses to dis-play His love to children is the institution of the family.

Your grandchild may have gone to his mother and father time after time, looking for that love, but he may have come back empty-handed. He may have almost given up on ever being loved—really loved. In his despair, he may be trying to fill the hole in his heart with drugs or alcohol, with sex or violence, with raunchy music or wild friends, with scholastic success or bully-ing his peers. All those pursuits are attempts to block pain and find the love he's always wanted.

But now he has come to you. He's on your doorstep. Maybe you're his last resort. What do you see when you open the door? Do you see a dirty, offensive, rebellious kid? Or do you see an incredibly valuable treasure? Your answer will determine your response at that pivotal moment in his life. But if your convictions about God's unconditional love for you spill out in actions of love toward him, his life will never be the same.

We have now examined five principles that help us be more effective influences in the lives of our grandchildren. In the next chapter we will examine some obstacles that may need to be overcome.

Reflection

1. Have you seen changes in our cultural values duringyour lifetime? What factors have caused those changes?

2. What are some examples of people (no names, please!) who have changed their behavior and values to suit a situation?

3. What are some examples of people you know who have held to their convictions no matter what it cost them?

4. What were the short-term and long-term consequences to the person making the decisions in both of the previous cases? What were the consequences to those watching?

5. What are some reasons it is good to explain to a child the benefits of doing right?

6. What are some ways the shift from "duty" to "rights" changed people's respect for authority?

7. Describe your generation's view of authority, your children's generation's view, and your grandchildren's view.

8. Why does it take strong convictions to love, forgive, and accept people?

9. How did your grandparents influence your spiritual life? Explain.

10. What are some ways you can impart spiritual wisdom to your grandchildren?

11. Read Paul's prayers in Ephesians 3:14-21, Philippians 1:9-11, and Colossians 1:9-14. How can these passages shape your prayers for your grandchildren?

12. What needs to happen in your own life to allow God's love and strength to "spill out" from you into the lives of others?

Don't Buy Their Defenses

"Try not to overreact to the Millennials' culture as your parents overreacted to yours!"—Dawson McAllister

I want to be close to her," a grandmother confided to me, "but when I try to talk to her, she seems to push me away." This dear lady was heartbroken. She had watched her granddaughter suffer through her parents' divorce, and she could see the pain and confusion written on the girl's face. She had watched as the girl tried to fill up the hole in her heart with all kinds of things, like loud music, loud clothes, and loud boys.

Now this concerned grandmother wondered if the girl's new friends were leading her down the wrong path. She had heard that one of them had been caught smoking marijuana, and they all had "that look" about them. The grandmother had tried to talk to her granddaughter, but the girl never seemed to have time. She was always in a hurry to get out of the house, away from her mother and brothers. And when the grandmother summoned the courage to ask about her hurts from the divorce, a topic none of them seemed to be able to talk about without explosions of anger and blaming each other, the girl froze and refused to even discuss it. The girl's defenses against exposing her pain were both ice and fire, the ice of cool detachment from talking about it, and fiery explosions of rage that screamed, "Stay away from me!" and intimidated anyone within earshot.

Children who are hurt and angry instinctively use defenses to protect themselves from being hurt again. The problem is that those defenses also prevent them from experiencing the love they so desperately want.

FENCES, BOMBS, AND SPONGES

Young people, like adults, protect themselves in a variety of ways. Some of their methods are subtle, but some are as plain as day. Some are terribly offensive, and others appear to be normal, acceptable behavior, yet hide deep insecurities.

The age and developmental stage of the child are also factors to consider. For example, younger children are often most visibly affected in times of trauma, but they are usually the most resilient and tend to bounce back when they receive love and care. Older children are more capable of interpreting the event and drawing conclusions about the extent of the damage to themselves and to others in the family. Some of them lash out in rage; others internalize their painful emotions.

Those who hide their hurt may seem to be doing quite well, but they are dying inside.

Those who hide their hurt may seem to be doing quite well, but they are dying inside. In addition, adolescence is a time when young people naturally

238

question and resist authority. During this emotionally delicate time, teenagers often interpret family traumas as intense, personal threats. Trust, already fragile, can easily be ruptured, and the emotional damage can be extensive.

When your grandchildren bristle in anger or withdraw when you offer to help, don't react too quickly, too negatively, or too personally. Younger children often accept help more eagerly, but even then, some of them resist for a while before they believe they can trust your love. As you observe your grandchildren, look beneath the surface. Beneath the anger, defiance, or isolation you see lies a wounded heart.

Let's look at a few of the defenses children use to protect themselves.

Fences

Some young people use fairly benign behaviors to keep others away. They stay busy, giving them an excuse to dodge meaningful conversations that could lead to the exposure of their hurt. They may be driven to succeed in school or sports, hoping to take their attention away from the pain in the family and win a bit of approval. Some hide behind humor, and they are funniest when things are tense. They hope that a few laughs will take away the pain, or at least give them a brief period of relief. Some young people become absorbed in music, television, or the computer. They spend endless hours escaping to a world away from the pain. Whenever they have to interact with others, the pain comes back and they quickly retreat to their private and safe cocoon of media.

In each case, the troubled young person may smile and look happy, hoping to communicate, "Hey, I'm fine. Don't bother to ask me any hard questions."

Bombs

When some young people are confronted after being hurt, or especially after doing something wrong, they become defiant and respond with a verbal blast: "I don't care what you think! Get out of my face!" While we wonder why they did something so foolish in the first place, they may be planning something even more outlandish. And we, of course, are astonished that they keep doing it again and again, suffering severe consequences each time.

One reason for such behavior is that they are proving they are tough. They have been hurt, perhaps deeply, but they're not going to cry about it. Just the opposite: they put themselves in situations time after time to prove they can take even worse from life than what they've experienced so far. If this pattern continues, they develop a reputation for toughness that is challenged by others who want to prove *they* are the toughest around, leading to fight after fight or increasingly foolish daredevil activities.

Others reserve their "explosions" for family members. They aren't proving they are tough. Instead, they are trying to hurt those who have hurt them, and they lash out violently at even the smallest infraction. Living with these kids can be very confusing because they act very calm and polite around their friends and anyone not perceived as a threat, but they may explode in rage

at a parent, grandparent, sibling, or teacher. They hope to not only inflict pain in retaliation, but also to intimidate the offending person—and anyone else who happens to see the pyrotechnics.

They hope to not only inflict pain in retaliation, but also to intimidate the offending person—and anyone else who happens to see the pyrotechnics.

Sponges

In contrast to the "bombs," other young people bottle up their hurts and never let them show. They soak up the pain in the family like a sponge, blaming themselves for anything and everything that has hurt anyone. Many are driven to please people in the family to win affection and find love. They become "puppets on a string," changing their behavior when they sense approval or rejection in even the slightest voice inflection or raised eyebrow.

Sponges are often very nice out of desperation to have people accept them. I know some children who are so nice they agree with everybody about everything. In fact, they are so agreeable that they can't offer an opinion about the most basic issues of life, something as simple as what kind of pizza to order, because they are afraid of offending anyone who might disagree with them. In many families where someone is acting out in out-of-control rage, the "sponges" are easily overlooked. The loud person usually gets all the attention, but the quiet, passive family members are just as desperate and needy.

Children learn these behaviors and use them for a reason: to keep people away and to prevent any more pain. And it works with a lot of grandparents.

But don't buy their defenses! Look around the fences, behind the bombs, and beneath the sponges to see what is really there. Realize that from the child's point of view, their attempts to avoid more hurt are not only reasonable, they are necessary. Don't criticize the child for protecting himself. Instead, do whatever it takes to win trust, which is the door to genuine love and healing.

If your grandchild is withdrawn or passive, go out of your way to encourage him. Find something he does well, and convince him to take a confident step or two. Passivity is fueled by fear, and often, by an unidentified fear. Many children have lived so long with their fears that they can't readily identify them any longer. As you spend time encouraging him patiently and persistently, he will learn to trust you, and he may allow you into a place in his heart that has long been locked. If so, take the opportunity to replace his fears with confidence and security.

Dominating, controlling children are also reacting to a deep sense of insecurity. But rather than cower, they demand to be in control. They have lost trust in other people to love them, meet their needs, and provide the warmth and safety they need. In response, they try to control themselves and other people.

When I was a boy, I wasn't a good athlete. Yet when we went outside for recess, I took control and claimed the role of being captain so I could pick my team. Was that demanding and bossy? Yes, of course. My behavior was a direct reaction to my athletic insecurity. If your

grandchild is demanding and controlling, don't respond only to his surface behavior. Try to identify the fear that is causing his behavior, and show unconditional love and understanding to relieve that underlying fear. Demanding children, like demanding adults, will be defensive and resistant because they don't want to give up control. Your patience and persistence will be put to the test with these children, but stay strong. Let your love be without end.

If your grandchild is rebellious, don't overreact. If your grandchild is accused of a crime or any other sin, get the facts. Many grandparents are too quick to either excuse or to blame. I've known grandparents who, when they were told a grandson was accused of destroying mailboxes with a baseball bat, jumped to conclusions. They instantly assumed the grandchild was guilty, and no amount of evidence would change their minds. Others would declare the boy's innocence even when confronted with surveillance cameras with indisputable photos of the boy doing the deed. "He was framed!" they cry. "It must be somebody who looks a lot like him. I know he'd never do anything like that."

> *If your grandchild is accused of a crime or any other sin, get the facts.*

In one case, a young man was caught selling drugs at school. The boy's grandmother called her pastor and protested, "That principal is trying to make him into something he's not. He would never do anything like selling drugs!" But the pastor knew her grandchild, and he knew enough to believe that the young man may well have been selling drugs. He tried to help the grand-mother see the pattern of behavior in the boy's life, but she steadfastly defended him. "Those other boys put those pills and that money in his backpack," she insist-ed. "I just know they did."

"What about the needle marks on his arms?"

"Oh, he got those scratches playing football."

"Football season has been over for three months."

"He's always been a slow healer."

Nothing the pastor said made a dent in this grand-mother's defenses, and as long as she excused him, she certainly wouldn't hold him accountable for his behav-ior. She saw her defense as an expression of love for him, but in reality, it prevented him from getting the help he desperately needed.

If your grandchild is accused of something, try to be as objective as possible to find out what really happened. Listen carefully, and be shrewd enough not to believe just one side of the story. Your explosive or rebellious grand-child is looking for love, too. Be sure to give it in full measure, but don't bail him out of the consequences of his behavior. Love helps people become responsible.

Your granddaughter may wear strange clothes, a tongue stud, and purple hair, but don't make a big deal of those things. She's trying to show her independence. She's making a statement that she's her own person. Instead, talk about her life, her hopes and dreams, and your own hopes and dreams. In other words, don't let her outward appearance affect your heart of love for her. Some grandparents believe that every young man who wears an earring is gay, and that every young woman who has a pierced navel is promiscuous. Don't jump to those conclusions. Many young people in the 60s wore long hair and bell-bottom jeans. Some of the people with that look were into drugs and sex, some were in the Jesus Movement, and some just liked the styles. It's not so different with today's fashions and fads.

But don't be naïve as you're gathering facts and as you avoid jumping to conclusions. Young people who feel ongoing emotional pain will try lots of things to feel better, and many will self-medicate to relieve the pain. Some use alcohol or drugs. Others turn to things we may not associate with self-medication to block the pain in their lives: food, television, pornography, sex, or busyness. Each of these can be a way to escape the intense hurt and anger the person feels, if only for a few minutes or a few hours.

Look for warning signs. The first stages of experimentation with addictive substances and behaviors are often followed by active and consistent involvement in those things. The rush of adrenaline, alcohol, or drugs gives the user a high, and the risk of being caught adds to the drama and excitement. Soon, the high becomes addictive, and the person organizes his life—his money, his time, and his relationships—around the behavior. He may lie to keep people from finding out what he is doing, and he may steal to feed his habit.

Watch for changes in eating and sleeping habits, new friends, physical lethargy, inconsistencies in stories, and irritability. Those signs may or may not signal an addiction, but they certainly warrant your concern. If you suspect your grandchild is self-medicating, talk to the parents, and get help from a pastor or a Christian counselor. And never stop loving that dear child, no matter how many lies he tells. Realize that he is still looking for love, peace, and acceptance, and you may be his only hope.

And don't take for granted those nice and quiet grandchildren who are driven to please. They don't cause problems, so they are often overlooked. Take time to show you love them. Try to get beyond their high-walled defenses, their compulsion to hide, and their fear of arguments or even of attention. Talk about your own childhood and the stresses you faced. As you show you are genuine and that you care, they may let down their defenses and relax a bit. Encourage them to express their own opinions, to muster the courage to disagree from time to time, and to develop their own identity.

And don't take for granted those nice and quiet grandchildren who are driven to please.

Each of these types of defenses has a common root of fear and insecurity, but the remedies are quite different. You will need insight and wisdom to perceive the problem accurately and help each person take the next step toward confidence and hope.

MISSED OPPORTUNITIES

"I just don't understand him," a grandmother said of her grandson as she grimaced and shook her head. Then she lowered her voice: "And to be honest, I don't even like being around him." This refined older lady prided herself on her status in the community. She was known for her roses, her antiques, her regular Wednesday afternoon bridge parties, and her emotional control. Her junior high grandson didn't care a whit about the flowers, her old furniture, or the gaggle of old women who gathered in the living room on Wednesdays, but her emotional distance left him feeling alone. That mattered.

The boy had tried to make connections with his grandmother, and she responded politely—always politely, never with the unbridled enthusiasm of a person who is thrilled to be with someone she loves. As the boy entered adolescence and did the things most boys do in those years, her demeanor became more condemning and less polite. She tried to correct him from time to time, but she hadn't earned the right to speak to his heart. When he ignored her, she huffed as she walked away, "He is the most impudent young man I have ever known!" He wasn't sure what "impudent" meant, but he had a good idea it wasn't a compliment.

The grandmother's friends, of course, agreed with her assessment of the boy's behavior and attitude, though they talked about him as little as possible to avoid embarrassing her any more. Her daughter, the boy's mother, tried to intervene and bring the two together. She suggested her mother could be a bit more pleasant and a bit less critical. "After all," she told her mother, "he's just a boy. I think you'd really enjoy him if you . . . well, if you found something to like about him."

But her mother replied, "In my day, no child would be allowed to act the way he does. My grandmother would have given me the spanking of my life if I talked to her the way that young man [she didn't call him by name when she was angry] talks to me. No, he needs a firm hand. Yours *and* mine." Instead of building a bridge, the mother only got a taste of the criticism her son had been experiencing.

Like this grandmother, some of us miss wonderful opportunities to have a powerfully positive impact on our grandchildren. Other factors always push us away from our grandchildren, such as distance, resistance from them or from the parents, or not understanding what makes them tick. But the obstacles usually can be overcome if we are creative and try hard enough. Below are some of the most common reasons we don't get involved.

We are intimidated.

Frankly, certain youthful behavior scares us, and it's easier to just avoid it altogether. One grandfather tried to help his grandson who had been caught shoplifting, but the young man cursed him and pushed him down. While few of us have experienced physical harm from a grandchild, many have been the brunt of yelling, cursing, and door slamming.

We are afraid of being ineffective.

Some of us aren't afraid a grandchild will hurt us physically or emotionally, but we don't have confidence we can make a difference. In an age of specialists, parents often turn to psychologists, psychiatrists, or social workers who are skilled to handle particular disorders. We can't even pronounce the diagnosis, and we sure don't have the skill to resolve the problem! We simply don't feel equipped to step into a child's life and provide the quality of help he needs.

But in reality, if we are available and we truly care, we can't help but make a difference. We don't need a degree in psychology or full knowledge of the problems and labels. We only need to be persistent in showing up and showing love.

> *We simply don't feel equipped to step into a child's life and provide the quality of help he needs.*

We experience resistance from the parents.

Some grandparents try to help, but are told by their child and the child's spouse, "Butt out!" And some are simply ignored. It's a difficult and frustrating position for such grandparents. We listen to friends talk about the wonderful relationships they have with their grandchildren, and our hearts are broken because we feel excluded for one reason or another. Perhaps we have stepped over the line and have given our advice once (or a thousand times) too often. Perhaps we have failed so miserably as parents that our assistance as grandparents isn't wanted. Or maybe our children have made such destructive decisions that they are embarrassed, and keeping us at a distance is a way of protecting their shattered egos.

We can't force compassion on anyone. That's not the way love works. We can only offer it and hope someone will accept it. If they don't, we can ask some questions to find out the reasons. Then, if the fault is ours, we can admit our errors and make amends to

rebuild the relationship. If the fault is theirs, we can forgive, love, and accept them, and try to build trust that
has been strained or broken.

We excuse ourselves.

Some grandparents feel, beyond any doubt, that
they know best when it comes to how to handle a problem with a grandchild. It may be the kid's fault, it may
be the parents' fault, but if anyone needs to change, we
are sure it's not us! And during our assessment, if we are
critical, distant, nosey, or exhibit any other behavior that
is less than helpful, we excuse ourselves because our
crusty behavior has served us well for decades.

I talked to a lady not long ago who told me how she
had viciously condemned a granddaughter who was
struggling after her brief marriage failed. The grandmother's words and the tone of her voice would have
made your toenails curl. This lady goes to church every
week, so I chided her, "Ma'am, I know you disapprove
of your daughter's choices, but do you think that's the
way the Lord wants you to treat her?"

She retorted, "Well, it must be all right with God. He
made me this way, and this is just the way I am."

**We've raised children, and we don't want the respon-
sibility of raising any more.**

Some of us are tired—physically, mentally, and emotionally. We spent the best years of our lives raising our
children, and now we expect somebody to take care of
us, or at least allow us some peace and quiet. When our
own children are having problems with their kids, that's

their problem. We don't want to get involved. Christmas and Thanksgiving? That's fine. Birthdays? No problem. But getting into the mud of hurt and anger, of depression or drug abuse? No thanks!

We are bitter because our own needs haven't been met.

Senior adults come in two flavors: sweet and sour. Some of the most delightful people I have ever met are older adults, and some of the most crotchety I've ever known are seniors who never resolved the hurt and anger they have felt for many years. Seniors are either singing in the rain, or they are sitting home on a gorgeous spring day complaining that surely it's raining somewhere!

To be brutally honest, some of us don't want to get involved in relieving our grandchildren's pain because are too busy nursing our own hurts. We feel sorry for ourselves, and our bitterness focuses our attention on those who have hurt us, not on serving others who need our love. We can be polite to our grandchildren, but that's about the extent of our emotional capacity. If they need more, they will have to get it from somebody else. We may be able to hide our bitterness by smiling at people at church or in the neighborhood, but we can't hide it from our grandchildren. They see the truth behind our smiley mask.

We are following the model of our grandparents.

Some of us grew up in an age when "children were seen and not heard."

Some of us grew up in an age when "children were seen and not heard." That was the model of family relationships in our grandparents' homes, and that's the model we have replicated. One lady told me that when she was a child, she and her brother were never allowed to eat meals with her parents and grandparents. They had to sit at a different table, and woe to them if they made so much noise that an adult had to get up and tell them to be quiet! She told me, "Today my grandkids—not the parents or the grandparents—rule the roost. It's hard to relate to them when I was so compliant and they seem so demanding."

We are surprised and offended by today's young people and their loud music, language, and clothes. They wouldn't have gotten by with that years ago. We try as hard as we can to make today's children fit into the mold we once knew, but the harder we try, the more strained our relationship with them becomes.

All the previous reasons (and many more) keep us from getting involved with our grandchildren. Even though they may seem completely understandable and justified in the pressure of the moment, they prevent us from making a difference in the lives of young people who desperately need our love and care.

I have already encouraged you not to be fooled by the defenses raised by young people. Now I challenge you not to buy your own defenses, either. Notice your own tendencies to withdraw, to blame, or to make excuses to avoid getting involved. As you do, you become able to make choices of character, not convenience. No matter what it takes, choose to show your love to each of your grandchildren. Muster the courage to take steps that show you care.

THE DOCTOR IS IN

Doctors examine surface symptoms of a patient, but they are trained to look for the underlying source of the symptom. That's why they use X-rays, blood work, endoscopy, and every other conceivable test to determine the exact cause of the problem. Only then can they determine the appropriate treatment. They are very careful not to jump to conclusions and prescribe medicines or therapies too quickly.

I heard of a young man who had an itchy spot on his back. It was hard to reach, but he contorted his arm behind his back and applied some cortisone cream to it. The itch, however, didn't go away. After a few weeks, the spot became a bit sore. He went to the local pharmacy, and the pharmacist suggested he try a muscle relaxer. The man didn't understand how an itch could turn into a muscle ache, but he bought a tube and applied the medicine a couple of times each day.

Yet a few weeks later, the spot was even more painful. The man asked his brother to take a look at it, and in the spirit of most brothers, he took a quick glance and declared authoritatively, "Aw, it's nothing. It'll go away in a few days."

Months passed, and the young man tried every cream on the market. Still, nothing helped. In fact, the pain got worse. Finally, he talked to his brother again. The brother told him, "Are you still complaining about that place on your back? Let me take a look at it." When the man took his shirt off, his brother looked and exclaimed, "Uh oh."

"What do you mean?" asked the man.

"I mean that spot has gotten bigger . . . and blacker. I think you'd better go see a doctor real soon."

Two days later, the young man went to a dermatologist, who immediately concluded the spot was melanoma, a deadly form of skin cancer. After tests confirmed his diagnosis, surgery was scheduled as quickly as possible. And after surgery, the doctor told the young man, "I don't think we got it all. We tried, but it has spread quite a lot."

The next three months were emotionally and physically excruciating for the man. The cancer, indeed, had spread. The brother felt terrible as well because he had been so flippant those months before when the spot was much smaller, and perhaps, treatable. Three months after the surgery, the young man died. At the funeral, the brother reflected, "I wish I had paid more attention when he said the spot was sore. He wouldn't have asked me to take a look if he hadn't been concerned, but I guess I was preoccupied with other things. And to be honest, it never crossed my mind that it could really be that serious. When he came to me the second time, it was too late."

Grandchildren often have difficulties that they can't see themselves.

Grandchildren often have difficulties that they can't see themselves. If grandparents pay attention, and if they aren't preoccupied with their own needs, they may be able see the problem before it

3. Are you tempted to use any of the excuses listed in this chapter to avoid being involved in your grandchild's life? Review them and identify any that apply to you. Explain what you need to do to take steps to be more involved.

—We are intimidated.

—We are afraid of being ineffective.

—We experience resistance from the parents.

—We excuse ourselves.

—We've raised children, and we don't want the responsibility of raising any more.

—We are bitter because our own needs haven't been met.

—We are following the model of our grandparents.

4.   Is the doctor in? Explain your ability to diagnose the underlying causes of your grandchild's problems (if there are any).

What do you need to do to become a better "doctor"?

Hope for the Future

❦

*"Most ancient secular philosophers viewed hope as a temporary
illusion, and thus they had no hope. . . . When crises arose (as
they always do), human hope broke up 'like that house that is
built upon the sand.' Paul observed that those without Christ
grieved because they had no hope (I Thess 4:13). But the followers
of God have had hope from the beginning of biblical times. The
Hebrew word for hope means 'hopeful watching.' "
—Jimmy Long, in* Generating Hope

*P*urpose. Adventure. Hope. A person may be able to
exist without a vision for his future, but he can't
really live. Great goals galvanize our hearts and
thrill our souls. They give us incredible energy and enthusiasm, and they give us tenacity when times are tough.
This is true for you and your grandchild, and you can't
impart hope for the future unless you have it yourself.

THE SOURCE OF HOPE

Most people today, as in generations past, put their
hopes in things they can see but which cannot last,
things like money, possessions, fame, and power.
Television commercials and magazine ads scream at us
a million times a day that using a particular product or
service will satisfy our deepest longings. And maybe
those products will help . . . for a few minutes, or at best,
a few days.

However, God has made us so that nothing can ultimately satisfy us. Lasting fulfillment is found only in

God and His purposes. And what is God's purpose? The Scriptures tell us that all of history is pointing to a day when God will be revealed to the entire world and "every knee shall bow" before Him. On that day, wrongs will be righted and lies will be replaced with truth. In the meantime, our purpose is to prepare ourselves and those around us. It is an unspeakable privilege to advance the kingdom of God so that more people will love and follow Him.

As author Os Guinness stated so clearly in his book, *The Call*, the high calling of every human being is first to Someone, then to something, and finally, to somewhere. We are called to know and love Jesus Christ, to look to Him as our Master and Lord. Then God shows us how we can be involved in advancing His kingdom, as a missionary or as a mom, as a preacher or as a plumber. Everything we do can be a platform for honoring God and advancing His kingdom in the hearts of men and women, grandsons and granddaughters.

In *Generating Hope*, Jimmy Long wrote, "The Christian perspective of the future should include hope for ourselves and offering hope to others. This Christian hope is not synonymous with wish. Biblical hope assumes 'unconditional certainty.' "[16]

One of the elements of giving children and grandchildren "the blessing," as identified by Gary Smalley and John Trent, is "picturing a special future." By noticing a child's special skill or knowledge, we can then paint a word picture of how that talent might be developed and used to accomplish great things.

---

16 Long, *Generating Hope*, p. 116.

"Small goals," a wise man once said, "do not inflame the hearts of men." Picturing a special future for your grandchild paints a large goal and inflames his heart to strive toward great things, especially if those goals are connected in some way to the ultimate goal of honoring God and advancing His kingdom.

> *"Small goals," a wise man once said, "do not inflame the hearts of men."*

A friend has a grandson who is a gifted artist. When the boy was in grade school, my friend often talked to the boy about his drawings and paintings, asking questions and encouraging him. Now the boy is a young man, and my friend is still very much involved in his grandson's life. They talk about his art, but more pointedly, about the possibilities for the young man's future. My friend paints his own pictures with words that help the young man envision how he might excel by combining his artistic talent with his interest in youth ministry and missions. Recently, he told his grandson, "You know, I think you'd make a fantastic art professor in college. You could sure teach students a lot about painting and sculpture, but more than that, you could go on mission trips with them in the summer and at spring break! Man, what an impact you could have on those kids. They'd be so lucky to have you as their prof!" No one knows what is in that young man's future, but his vision has been expanded by his grandfather's word portrait. Instead of seeing his talent only as a way to make money, he now sees it as a vehicle to advance God's kingdom and have a powerful impact on people.

Each of us knows people who live without hope. They trudge through the routines of life with little joy. After a while, their goal is to escape pain, not to accomplish anything meaningful. Relationships become stiff and distant, nothing is exciting, and negative thoughts cloud their minds. Theologian Jurgen Moltmann observed, "Living without hope is no longer living. Hell is hopelessness and it is not for nothing that at the entrance to Dante's hell there stands the words: 'Abandon hope, all you who enter here.'"[17]

You may be the best, and perhaps the only, source of hope for your grandchild. Everyone else in his life may be out of control or criticizing him, and everything else in his life may be turning to ashes. But you are a light in the darkness. You have the incredible privilege of offering hope to one who is hopeless in an empty and painful world. For hope to pour out and drench your grandchild, you must have your own ample supply.

God may not rescue us out of our trouble. More often, He rescues us through our trouble by teaching us deep lessons we would not learn any other way.

It's so easy to get caught up in all the pain, the confusion, and the foolish decisions of your grandchildren and their parents—to think, "Oh, what's the use? They'll never learn." Rise above that despair by riveting your own sight on a God who is both good and sovereign, one who is wise and powerful. God may not rescue us out of our trouble. More often, He rescues us *through* our trouble by

17 Jurgen Moltmann, *Theology of Hope,* (Fortress, Minneapolis, Minnesota, 1993), p. 32

teaching us deep lessons we would not learn any other way. That perspective is true for us and for each member of our families, and it is true whether our grandchildren are suffering tremendous stress, only a normal amount, or if they are doing quite well.

Faith in a good and sovereign God gives us hope that every joy and every trial is soft clay in the hands of the Potter who loves us enough to make something good out of our pain and suffering—if we will only trust Him. He seldom accomplishes these rich blessings quickly. Instead, like the potter, He takes His time to prepare the clay, to turn it gently and firmly, and to use fire to confirm the shape and make it useful. That's the best possible potential for a lump of clay, and that's the hope of a broken, shapeless life.

WHATEVER IT TAKES

A grandparent's hope inspires the courage to step in and make a difference in a grandchild's life, whatever it takes. When I was growing up, the Superintendent of Education for Morgan County was a wonderful man named George Nancarrow. His wife was the secretary of the school I attended. They had two daughters, Beth and Donna, who were a little older than I was. The younger daughter, Donna, went to college and married a wonderful Christian. She and her husband, Rob, spent several years working on a college campus with Campus Crusade for Christ.

In time, Rob and Donna moved to our area, got teaching jobs, and adopted a child named Camp. When Camp was only four months old, Donna was exposed to a powerful bacteria and her condition quickly deteriorated. One night she gave a devotional at a PTA meeting, and within 24 hours she had died, leaving her husband with a small child.

The Nancarrows knew Rob was totally committed to the welfare of his son, but they were eager to help him any way they could. They lived nearby, so they could be there for the boy when his dad needed their assistance. They didn't want the tragedy of Donna's death to be a deterrent to Camp's well-being, so they made a choice to be committed and involved in his life.

And their efforts have paid enormous dividends. Camp has grown both physically and emotionally. He knows he is loved, and he has one of the healthiest self-concepts of anyone I've ever seen. The Nancarrows could have said, "Our beloved daughter is dead, and our son-in-law can take care of the boy by himself. Besides, we've worked hard all our lives, and we deserve to have time for ourselves now." But they didn't say that. Instead, they made a conscious, considered decision to be involved in the life of their grandchild.

The Nancarrows demonstrate three simple but profound steps for providing an environment of hope for grandchildren. These steps are:

1. Make a considered commitment to be involved.

Imparting hope doesn't happen by accident. It requires clear thinking and a rock-solid commitment to get involved in the life of a grandchild. This kind of commitment may involve sacrifice, but caring for grandchildren enriches your life so much that you will consider your time with them one of the greatest privileges you have experienced. It isn't always easy, but careful consideration at the beginning prevents you from being surprised by any of the difficulties that may occur.

Listen for the moments your grandchildren share their joy, and for the times they share their hurts. Anytime a child says, "Grandmama, guess what?" you can be sure you have a terrific opportunity to connect.

2. Be your grandchild's biggest cheerleader.

Parents may gripe at her, friends may make fun of her, teachers may scold her, and siblings may bother her, but you can be your granddaughter's most outspoken fan and biggest cheerleader. Look for every opportunity to speak words of hope and courage, to show love and joy in her presence, and to express your affection in ways that correspond with her love language. Let her see the sheer delight in your eyes when you look at her, and let her find great strength in your belief that God has a wonderful purpose for her life.

> *You can be your granddaughter's most outspoken fan and biggest cheerleader.*

3. Keep loving through thick and thin.

You may be confused about the best ways to demonstrate your love, but don't stop. The parents may not appreciate your efforts to give hope to a child whom they've given up on, but don't quit. The grandchild may resist your attempts to love her, but keep at it. When you become discouraged and are tempted to give up, stay involved. These obstacles don't mean the grandchild doesn't need love; they indicate that he needs love more than ever. If you see obstacles as hopeless roadblocks, you'll give up. But if you can see them as cries for your help, you'll keep loving, giving, praying, and serving.

At some point, many of us will experience what Henry Blackaby, the author of *Experiencing God*, calls "a crisis of commitment." We have done everything we know to do, but nothing has helped. We have every reason to quit, and everything inside us tells us it's time to throw in the towel. When that happens, remember this: By the time a grandparent is tempted to quit on a child, every other adult and institution has probably already given up on him. Parents, siblings, the school, and the police may have given up hope for that child. There is no one else. The grandparent is very likely the last hope for help, stability, and growth. When you are the last person holding on to the rope, don't let go.

LENNIE CROSS

My grandmother, Lennie Cross, is a wonderful and loving lady. She was from a very poor, large, rural family. She had little education, and she married when she and my grandfather were both very young. When he died in his mid-40s, she was left with several children and a number of bills, but no source of income.

She and the children lived in a rented home. Life was hard. Years later, after the three older boys had grown and moved away, she got a job in the lunchroom at a local school.

Through all those difficult years, people who knew my grandmother were well aware they must follow one cardinal rule: Never criticize, but always look for the good in people. Her positive, thankful spirit pervaded every event and every relationship, and her family learned from her example. Others may have had their own opinions, to be sure. But if they said they didn't like the pudding, they still wouldn't criticize the cook.

When my grandfather died, the only asset my grandmother had was her positive outlook on life. If she had allowed herself and her children to be absorbed with their problems instead of rising above them, our family legacy would be far different than it is today. Each of her children grew up to be successful adults with loving, supportive families, in many ways a testimony to her indomitable spirit.

"Big Mother" (that's what all her grandchildren call her) has always been very affirming toward me. Whenever I speak, she comments on something she liked about my talk. She still writes me notes of appreciation, even though today her handwriting is very frail. On every birthday since I can remember, she has given me a dollar bill. I still have every one of them, and I treasure them more than anyone can imagine. She may have never heard a talk on love languages, but she is a master of all of them. She communicates love in every conceivable way.

One of the things that means a lot to me is that when I go to see her, she stops whatever she is doing and gives me her full, undivided attention as long as I'm there. No matter how busy or how involved she may be in a project, she considers me to be more important. And, of course, it's not just me. She gives the same love and attention to anyone who visits her. She knows I love boiled okra and sliced tomatoes, so if she has even the slightest notion that I might be coming to see her near a mealtime, she cooks what she knows I love to eat. We don't eat what she prefers. She loves me so much that she cooks what makes *me* happy. That's love!

Over the years, I've seen my grandmother's optimism tested. She has buried two grandchildren, and those tragedies have broken her heart. Other grandchildren have done things that embarrassed her, and it wasn't easy for her to deal with those situations. In every case, though, she made the hard choice to keep loving, to keep believing, and to keep hoping that good would come out of difficulties.

> *In every case, though, she made the hard choice to keep loving, to keep believing, and to keep hoping that good would come out of difficulties.*

I didn't understand the full significance of her role in my own life until Debbie and I had Maegan and Melodi. As I watched my parents and in-laws shape my girls' lives, I got a lot more insight about how my grandmother had shaped my life so positively.

When my grandmother hears her friends criticizing their grandkids, she jumps in and corrects them, "Let me tell you something, you're talking about your family. Stop being so critical of them. Love them and stand by them no matter what they've done." Gossip is not a virtue, and my grandmother doesn't tolerate it.

R EFLECTION

1. What are the hopes and dreams of most people you know?

   Which of these desires focus on things that will pass away, and which are based on eternal things?

2. Describe a time in your life when your sense of purpose and meaning was very clear and strong.

3. Describe your sense of hope today (the source, the strength, and the impact it has on you and others).

4. Think of each of your grandchildren. How can you paint a picture of hope for each one's future?

5. Write a prayer for each of your grandchildren. Consider the child's talents, specific needs, spiritual life, and sense of purpose. You might want to go back to the Reflection section at the end of Chapter 8 and reexamine the passages of Scripture to shape your prayer.

Leaving a Legacy

One of the most important things a grandparent can do in life is pass along a legacy of hope and courage to a grandchild. Chapter 7, "The Connection Principle: Leaving a Legacy," provides principles and encouragement to communicate your story so your grandchildren—and generations to come—are inspired by your life's message.

Some grandparents have heard me speak on this topic, and they have shaken their heads and said sadly, "But I don't have an exciting story to tell." Your story may not compete with the movie thrillers in the theaters today, but your life contains a powerful message. Your successes tell of God's goodness, your failures tell of how much we all need God's grace, and the tragedies that you have experienced communicate that we can trust God even when we don't understand His ways. The issue is not just what happened in our lives, but more importantly, how we interpret them and allow God to use them to shape our attitudes and actions. In this age of demands for instant happiness and success, young people desperately need the wisdom and courage of family members who have faced adversity and grown from it.

Take time to think carefully about the important events in your life and how you interpreted them at the time. Then look back on them and try to find the lessons, perhaps hidden at the time of the events, that you can draw from them now. A compelling message doesn't just happen. That message, whether it is communicated in a quiet conversation, a family gathering, a book, an audiotape, or a video, is the product of careful reflection.

Let me offer some suggestions as you consider leaving a legacy to your grandchildren:

1. Draw a timeline of your life. Mark the important events, including the pleasant and the painful ones.

2. Describe your parents. What made them happy, sad, or angry? In what ways were they successful? How did they respond to failure and heartache? What role did they play in the important events in your timeline?

3. Describe your siblings. What made them happy, sad, or angry? In what ways were they successful? How did they respond to failure and heartache? What role did they play in the important events in your timeline?

4. What people, events, or activities in your life have given you the most pleasure and sense of accomplishment? Describe them. What lessons can you draw from those experiences?

5. What people, events, or activities have brought you the most pain? Describe them. How did you interpret and respond to them at the time? What insights have you gained over the years about those painful times?

Using
The Grandparent Factor
in Classes and Groups

This book is designed for individual study, classes, and small groups. The most powerful way to absorb and apply these principles is for each person to study and consider the application questions individually, then to discuss them in either a class or a group environment.

Your church my want to conduct a class on Sunday mornings during the Bible Study hour, or perhaps on a weekday evening. A pastor or another skilled communicator can teach these principles over 8 to 12 weeks. Of course, the nature of our relationships with our grandchildren is complex and difficult, so it may take more than one time through the material for people to grasp and apply some of the points. That's entirely understandable and appropriate. I suggest that your church conduct these classes back to back over the course of the year. In most cases, those who go through the material once will want to go through it again because their first exposure will raise many questions they want answered.

The questions and exercises at the end of each chapter should promote reflection, application, and discussion. Order enough copies of the book for each person to have one of their own. For couples, I strongly encourage both to have their own book so they can record their individual thoughts and prayers.

A recommended schedule for a class might be:

Week 1	Introduction to the material. The teacher can tell his own story, share his hopes for the group, and provide books for each person
Week 2	Chapter 1
Week 3	Chapter 2
Week 4	Chapter 3
Week 5	Chapter 4
Week 6	Chapter 5
Week 7	Chapter 6
Week 8	Chapter 7
Week 9	Chapter 8
Week 10	Chapter 9
Week 11	Chapter 10
Week 12	Questions and Answers: specific questions that people want to talk about

Phil Waldrep

is a man with a heart for people. His passion to share the gospel and provide resources for believers to grow in their relationship with God began when he was a young man.

Phil gave his life to Jesus Christ when he was seven years old. Nurtured by the faith of the rural Baptist church he and his parents attended, Phil began seeking God for his guidance in choosing a career. He then realized the Lord was calling him to full-time ministry.

By age eighteen, Phil was speaking regularly in churches across the South. He formed the Phil Waldrep Evangelistic Association in 1980 to broaden his ministry and fulfill his vision.

© Charles Seifried

Today,

Phil receives numerous requests to speak. His yearly schedule includes invitations to many of the leading churches across North America. A leading expert on senior adult issues, he enjoys interacting with and communicating to that audience. Each year, Phil speaks to dozens of senior adult conventions, leads churches in senior adult revivals, and addresses many of the leading organizations and corporations in the world. His unique blend of humor, insight and communication skills make him a repeat guest.

Phil married the former Debbie Gray in 1984. They have two daughters, Maegan and Melodi, and make their home in Decatur, Alabama. He is a graduate of the University of Alabama and the Luther Rice Theological Seminary.

If you would like to know more about Phil Waldrep Ministries or how you can have Phil speak to your church or organization, contact:

> Phil Waldrep Ministries
> P.O. Box 148
> Trinity, Alabama 35673-0148
> (256) 355-1554

© Charles Seifried

𝒫hil 𝒲aldrep Ministries

is a non-profit organization committed to sharing the gospel by every means, traditional and non-traditional, and to provide quality resources for believers to grow in their relationships with God, their families and their friends. In addition to books and tapes, the ministry conducts major conferences, including:

Senior Adult Celebrators!

Senior Adult Celebrators are events designed for retirees and senior adults. Held in major tourist areas, the Celebrators

© Charles Seifried

feature many of America's leading preachers, musicians, comedians and Christian celebrities. Among those who have appeared are Dr. David Jeremiah, Mark Lowry, George Beverly Shea, and Art Linkletter.

Women's Weekend Getaways

Women enjoy getting away with friends and focusing on their relationships with each other and the Lord. That is why the Women's Weekend Getaways are popular events for Christian women. The retreats begin on Friday night and conclude Sunday morning. They feature some of the most popular women speakers in the country.

Mountain Top Men's Retreat

Men from across the country gather each Spring for the Mountain Top Men's Retreat in Talladega, Alabama. The weekend event motivates men to develop their relationship with Christ, deepen their love for their family, and work more effectively in the local church.

Oasis Summer Student Camps & Student Celebrations!

Phil Waldrep Ministries joins hands with church youth ministers to provide a fun-filled, spiritually enriching week for high school and college students each summer. Oasis camps feature special guests, exciting worship, Bible studies and messages designed for today's teen. In addition, the camps feature special activities that cause teens to grow closer to God, their friends, family and church. The Student Celebrations! are designed to encourage and motivate students in their walk with God.

If you would like to know more about any of our exciting conferences, contact our office for a free brochure.

Phil Waldrep Ministries • (256) 355-1554

© Corbis

Tell us about your grandchild

Over the years, grandparents have told me wonderful stories about their grandkids. Some of those stories are included in this book, but of course, there simply isn't room in these pages for all the encouraging and heart-rending stories we hear.

Would you tell me about your grandchild? We may use those stories in a follow-up book or on our web site to encourage other grandparents to have a powerful impact on their grandkids. You can write to me at:

Phil Waldrep
Phil Waldrep Ministries
P.O. Box 148
Trinity, Alabama 35673-0148

Books make great gifts!
Order for yourself or a friend

The Grandparent Factor $19.95

Parenting Prodigals $19.95

Dinner on the Ground Cookbook $19.95

Fellowship Favorites Dessert Cookbook $12.00

Postage & handling (first book) **$4.00**

Postage & handling (each additional book) **$2.00**

If you wish to order by credit card call: (256) 355-1554
Make checks payable to Phil Waldrep Ministries
We accept: MasterCard, Visa, American Express, Discover

P.O. Box 148
Trinity, AL 35673-0148